# America's
# Trillion-Dollar
# Housing
# Mistake

HOWARD HUSOCK

# America's Trillion-Dollar Housing Mistake

*The Failure of*
*American Housing Policy*

**Ivan R. Dee**
*Chicago 2003*

Most of the contents of this book appeared originally in *City Journal*, published by The Manhattan Institute.

Library of Congress Cataloging-in-Publication Data:
Husock, Howard.
   America's trillion-dollar housing mistake : the failure of American housing policy / Howard Husock.
       p. cm.
   Most of the contents of this book originally appeared as articles in City Journal.
   Includes index.
   ISBN 1-56663-531-4
       1. Housing policy—United States. 2. Public housing—United States. 3. Community development corporations—United States. 4. United States. Dept. of Housing and Urban Development. I. Title: Trillion-dollar housing mistake. II. City Journal (New York, N. Y.) III. Title.

HD7293.H87 2003
363.5'85'0973—dc                                           2003055115

# Contents

# Introduction

For more than six decades, the United States has built public housing projects and otherwise subsidized housing for the poor. Everyone knows how quickly these housing projects, particularly in big cities, turn into dangerous, demoralized slums. But the problems with our low-income housing policy go much deeper than the unwholesome living conditions they provide. This book argues that our low-income housing policy is a mistake—over the decades, a trillion-dollar mistake—that, like so many other misguided anti-poverty programs, has harmed those it set out to help and has caused serious, and continuing, collateral damage in our cities.

I begin in Chapter One by debunking the key assumption behind all federal housing programs—that the market cannot provide housing for the poor. Far from being stuck in slums before the advent of public housing, upwardly mobile low-income Americans took advantage of a cornucopia of decent, sturdy, inexpensive, privately built homes—ranging from the three-deckers of Boston to the four-flats of Chicago to the bungalows of Oakland.

In Chapter Two I describe both the visible and invisible damage public housing causes to cities. Poor maintenance and high crime, radiating outward from projects overwhelmingly dominated by single-parent households, drive down property values in surrounding neighborhoods. Just as bad, public housing creates a "frozen city": the land and properties that subsidized housing occupies are permanently unavailable for new uses—whether for new homes or for new businesses—that could help those of all income levels. In New York City, for instance, public housing projects occupy the equivalent of 156 World Trade Center sites.

Recognizing how disastrous big housing projects like Chicago's Robert Taylor Homes are to the well-being of their residents and to the health of cities, housing officials and advocates have in recent years devised a series of alternatives. But as the next three chapters extensively describe, all of these new forms of housing assistance perpetuate the chronic problems in different ways. Chapter Three considers housing vouchers—government checks given to low-income households to pay private housing rent. This "Section 8" program, I show, frequently exports the social problems of inner-city public housing to working-class neighborhoods, whose residents have struggled to leave those problems behind. Opposition to the program is hardly racist: working-class African-American households are among those most upset.

Not all of these ill-advised new housing programs take the form of direct subsidies. The federal Community Reinvestment Act has forced mortgage lenders to make credit available to inner-city neighborhoods. But as Chapter Four notes, the loans, channeled through left-wing activist groups, have often gone on too-easy terms to those with spotty credit histories, and a disproportionate number of these loan recipients have let their properties deteriorate or have been delinquent on their mortgage payments. Like Section 8 vouchers, the CRA has hurt hardworking, upwardly mobile lower-income families by weakening working-class neighborhoods, where the CRA mortgages tend to be located.

Like housing vouchers, nonprofit Community Development Corporations are touted as a new and better way to provide housing for the poor and to revitalize cities. In Chapter Five I explain how they are just old wine in a new bottle. Far from being the indigenous bootstrap organizations they portray themselves to be, these CDCs rely on special funds that federal tax policy makes available to them—not on real private investment. And the housing they've built is quickly turning out to have many of the same problems as public housing projects.

If public housing addresses a nonexistent need—a fictional scarcity of affordable housing for poor families—and has instead become the last major vestige of a federal welfare system that helps perpetuate an underclass of poor, single-parent families, we ought to phase it out, as a system that does more harm than good, however unintentionally. As Chapter Six argues, we must make our housing policy consistent with the spirit of welfare reform. This means that we should not give the low-income single mothers who dominate housing projects a subsidized apartment for as long as they would like to stay there, at the same time we are trying to limit dependency by setting a time limit on other forms of public assistance. Charlotte, North Carolina, I show, has blazed a trail in understanding this crucial need for time limits in public housing assistance.

At the same time that we dismantle our public housing system, there is much we can do to ensure an ample supply of privately built affordable housing. Chapter Seven looks at Habitat for Humanity, the fast-growing nonprofit organization with branches throughout America and around the world. The group believes that the best way to house low-income families isn't to herd them into public housing but to design good new private houses that are inexpensive to build. And, in trying to help those of modest means, the group has identified various ways—including church attendance and a willingness to help others (though these are not the only indexes of good character)—to judge whether individuals are likely to be the kind of homeowners who make their payments and contribute to their neighborhoods.

I have developed these themes in the pages of *City Journal*, where these chapters originally appeared, over the last several years, and it is deeply gratifying to find that they are beginning to influence national policy. The Bush administration's Department of Housing and Urban Development has started to push for changes in housing policy that are consistent with the themes of this book. In the spring of 2003, for instance, the administration proposed to rename the housing voucher program Housing Assistance for Needy Families (echoing welfare reform's new name, Temporary Assistance for Needy Families) and to allow states to impose public housing time limits. And it has proposed, too, to curtail funding for the ill-advised HOPE VI program of simply replacing the old blighted housing projects with new mixed-income developments, described in Chapter Two.

Those who care about improving the health of the nation's cities—and helping the poor gain independence and a foothold on the ladder of social mobility—should applaud these moves. They promise to undo, step by step, our trillion-dollar public housing mistake.

H. H.

*Boston*
*May 2003*

# America's
# Trillion-Dollar
# Housing
# Mistake

# ONE

· · · · · · · · · · · · · · · · · · · · · · · · · · · · · · · · · · · · · · · · · · · · · · · ·

# We Don't Need
# Subsidized Housing

It's a scene that has been repeated time and again in recent years, but it still seems almost too perfectly symbolic to be true. Clinton Secretary of Housing and Urban Development Henry Cisneros turns up to preside over the demolition of yet another "severely distressed" public housing project. But his speech directs attention away from what is actually happening. Just before the scarred blocks of apartments tumble down in a puff of smoke—such unequivocal failures that they aren't worth preserving—the secretary confidently paints a vision of improved design and management that will make a new generation of government-supported housing work out. Sure, we've flopped so far, the message goes—but give us one more chance and we'll finally get it right.

But maybe the whole idea is wrong. Maybe our housing programs haven't failed because of some minor management problem but because they are flawed at the core. The truth is, devoting government resources to subsidized housing for the poor—whether in the form of public housing or even housing vouchers—is not just unnecessary but also counterproductive. It not only derails what the private market can do on its own, but, more important, it has profoundly destructive unintended consequences. For housing subsidies undermine the efforts of those poor families who work and sacrifice to advance their lot in life—and who have the right and the need to distinguish themselves, both physically and psychologically, from those who do not share their solid virtues.

Rather than confront these harsh truths, we have over the past century gone through at least five major varieties of subsidized housing, always looking for the philosophers' stone that will turn a bad idea into one that will work. We began with philanthropic housing built by "limited dividend" corporations, whose investors were to accept a below-market return in order to serve the poor. The disappointing results of such efforts—the projects served few people and tended to decline quickly—led housing advocates to call for public, not just private, spending for housing. Government first responded to their pleas with housing projects owned and operated by public authorities. These speedily declined. "Housers" then sought other solutions, such as using cheap, federally underwritten mortgages and rents paid by Washington to subsidize private landlords.

The expense of this last approach, which had its heyday in the 1960s, and the resultant wave of decline and foreclosure led to the twin approaches of our current era. In the first of these, tenants use portable, government-provided vouchers to pay any private landlord who will accept them.

In the second, federal tax credits encourage deep-pocketed corporate investors looking for tax shelters to finance new or renovated rental housing owned and managed by non-profit community groups. Both approaches have had serious problems, but this hasn't deterred housing advocates from asserting that the way to fix the housing market is through even more such subsidies than the $12 billion that HUD already provides (out of its $25 billion annual budget) and the billions more in subsidies that state and local governments expend.

This mountain of government housing subsidies rests on three remarkably tenacious myths.

Myth No. 1: *The market will not provide.* The core belief of housing advocates is that the private market cannot and will not provide adequate housing within the means of the poor. The photos of immigrants squeezed into postage-stamp-size rooms in a recent *New York Times* series on housing for the poor strain to make this point. But housers have been making such assertions for more than sixty years, and reality keeps contradicting them. In 1935, for example, Catherine Bauer—perhaps America's most influential public housing crusader—claimed that the private housing market could not serve fully two-thirds of Americans, and they would need public housing. The post–World War II era's explosion of home ownership quickly gave the lie to such claims, certainly with respect to those in the lower middle class and up.

As for the poor, a look at pre-depression history shows that housing advocates get it wrong again. From the end of the Civil War until the New Deal and the National Housing Act of 1937, which gave public housing its first push, the private housing market generated a cornucopia of housing forms to accommodate those of modest means as they gradually improved their condition. In those years Chicago saw the construction of 211,000 low-cost two-family homes—or 21 percent of its residences. In Brooklyn 120,000 two-family structures with ground-floor stores sprang up. In Boston some 40 percent of the population of 770,000 lived in the 65,376 units of the city's three-decker frame houses, vilified by housing reformers.

These areas of low-cost, unsubsidized housing were home to the striving poor. In Boston, as pioneer sociologists Robert Woods and Albert Kennedy describe it in their brilliant 1914 work, *The Zone of Emergence*, these neighborhoods teemed with clerks and skilled and semiskilled workmen. "Over 65 percent of the residence property of the zone is owned by those who reside on it," wrote Woods and Kennedy, "and this is the best possible index that can be given of the end that holds the imagination and galvanizes the powers of a large proportion of the population. Doubtless the greater share of this property is encumbered with mortgage, but it is an index of striving and accomplishment."

Even in the poorest neighborhoods, housing, if modest, was rarely abject. A 1907 report by the U.S. Immigration Commission, for instance, found that in Eastern cities, crowding in such neighborhoods was by no means overwhelming, with 134 persons for every 100 rooms. "Eighty-four in every one hundred of the homes studied are in good or fair condition," wrote the commission. True, many lived without hot water or their own bathrooms. But rents were cheap. A 1909 study by the President's Homes Commission of Washington, D.C., found that a majority of the twelve hundred families surveyed paid just 17.5 percent of their income for housing costs. Many of the poor—just like the "emerging" class that Woods and Kennedy described—lived in small homes they owned or in small buildings in which the owner lived.

To be sure, as we know above all from Jacob Riis's powerful 1891 book, *How the Other Half Lives*, some families lived in hovels, even in unlit cellars. "It no longer excites even passing attention when the sanitary police count 101 adults and 91 children in a Crosby Street house," he wrote, "[o]r when a midnight inspection in Mulberry Street unearths 150 'lodgers' sleeping on filthy floors in two buildings." Many buildings did not have their own toilets, and large numbers of people relied on public baths to get clean.

But it is essential to remember that the conditions in which these poor families lived were not permanent—a fact unacknowledged by either Riis or present-day housing advocates. After all, the generation of children for whom Riis despaired went on to accomplish America's explosive economic growth after the turn of the century and into the twenties. By 1930 the New York settlement-house pioneer Lillian Wald would write in her memoirs of the Lower East Side that, where once Riis had deplored overcrowding, she now found herself surrounded by "empties": the poor had climbed the economic ladder and headed to Brooklyn and the Bronx. In other words, "substandard" housing was a stage through which many passed but in which they did not inevitably remain. The arrival of Dominicans from Washington Heights in Hudson River Valley towns and Salvadorans from Queens on Long Island is proof that this process continues.

Perversely, housing reformers invariably make matters worse by banning the conditions that shock them. Insisting unrealistically on standards beyond the financial means of the poor, they help create housing shortages, which they then seek to remedy through public subsidies. Even Jacob Riis observed in 1907 that new tenement standards threatened "to make it impossible for anyone not able to pay $75 a month to live on Manhattan Island."

Although Riis's colleague Lawrence Veiller, head of the influential New York–based National Housing Association from 1900 to 1920, cautioned that "housing legislation must distinguish between what is desirable and what is essential," most housing programs since the New Deal have rejected this sensible advice. The high standards that have resulted—whether for the number of closets, the square feet of kitchen counter space, or handicapped access—have caused private owners and builders to bypass the low-income market. So stringent are the standards that, under current building codes and zoning laws, much of the distinctive lower-cost housing that shaped the architectural identity of America's cities—such as Brooklyn's attached brownstones with basement apartments—could not be built today.

True, even with relaxed building and housing codes, we still might not be able to build brand-new housing within the reach of those earning the minimum wage or those living on public assistance. Yet this is not an irresistible argument for government subsidies. Used housing, like used cars, gets passed along to those of more and more modest means. When new homes are built for the lower middle class, the rental housing in which they've been living (itself probably inherited from the middle class) historically has been passed along to those who are poorer.

In a subtle way, the very existence of subsidized housing

is likely to contribute to the overregulation that leads to constraints in housing supply—and to calls for further subsidies. When builders have plenty of work putting up high-cost subsidized apartments, they don't agitate for a less regulated market. Why should they seek an opportunity to build lower-margin low-cost housing? The rejoinder, then, to the myth that the market will not provide is that a greater supply of housing could be—and has been—created in a less regulated market.

Myth No. 2: *By taking profit-driven landlords out of the equation, state-supported housing can offer the poor higher-quality housing for the same rent.* Four generations of attempts to provide subsidized housing built to higher standards than the poor could afford on their own in the private market have proved that this idea just doesn't work. Each generation has seen the same depressing pattern: initial success followed by serious decline and ultimately by demands for additional public funds to cover ever-rising costs.

You can see the outlines of this pattern as early as 1854, when the New York Association for Improving the Condition of the Poor decided to build a "model tenement" at the corner of Elizabeth and Mott streets. Constructed by a newly formed limited-dividend corporation, the building degenerated just eleven years later into what would be called "one of the worst slum pockets in the city." It was sold and soon after demolished.

Like its ill-fated predecessor, later public housing also aimed to do away with profit, financing construction through the sale of public bonds and then using the project's rental income to pay a public authority to provide maintenance. But the maintenance failures of public housing projects became legendary, to the point that a 1988 study estimated it would take at least $30 billion to remedy them. Instead of providing housing that rental income from tenants can maintain, the federal government has had to supply $4 billion in annual "operating assistance" to housing authorities for maintenance and administrative costs—and still the maintenance problems multiply.

The new public housing model that advocates favor retains the core—and fatal—dogma that the profit motive has no place in providing housing for the poor. In this model, nonprofit community groups run smaller, mixed-income apartment buildings, financed by monies raised through the Low Income Housing Tax Credit, a program set up in 1986 to encourage corporations to support low-income housing. In New York City some 200 nonprofit groups manage 48,000 housing units. Although at this point such housing is widely viewed as successful, the New School for Social Research has found, in an examination of thirty-four developments in six cities, that "beyond an initial snapshot of well-being loom major problems which, if unaddressed, will threaten the stock of affordable housing in this study." Predictably enough, more than 60 percent of the projects already had trouble maintaining their paint and plaster, elevators, hall lighting, and roofs.

Why does nonmarket housing founder? First, providing the poor with better housing than they can afford also saddles them with higher maintenance costs than they can afford. A newly announced state-financed "affordable housing" complex in Cambridge, Massachusetts, will cost $1.3 million—for eight units. That's $162,500 per apartment. Recent subsidized projects in the Bronx and central Harlem cost $150,000 and $113,000 per unit, respectively.

These apartments may be built to higher standards, but their fancier kitchens, more numerous bathrooms, and larger space mean more maintenance. Not surprisingly, limited rents can't keep up with the need for service. The New York City Housing Partnership, which arranges private construction of housing for low-income buyers, has observed that nonprofit housing management groups in general "have no magic formula that allows them to manage property at less than cost. Ultimately they will need operating subsidies to remain viable."

Second, it is by no means true that cutting out the profit-making landlord reduces maintenance costs. On the contrary, public authorities and nonprofit management firms are bureaucracies with their own overhead expenses, and unlike private owners they have no incentive to control costs. Nor have their employees any incentive to provide good service; and tenants, who are not full-fledged paying customers, have little leverage. Indeed, public housing authorities have demonstrated an ability rivaling any slumlord to disinvest in their properties.

Rather than being a source of ill-gotten gains, private ownership is a source of cost control. The expensive but ineffective maintenance regime of subsidized housing—with its formal bids and union contracts—replaces housing maintenance performed through a far less costly informal economy. Poor homeowners and so-called tenement landlords (owners of small, multi-family buildings, many owner-occupied) contribute their own "sweat equity" or hire neighborhood tradesmen, not all of whom are licensed, let alone unionized. As one study of a low-income neighborhood in Montreal observed, "Owners can maintain their buildings and keep their rents low through the cooperation of their tenants on maintenance and through their own hard work." None of these factors comes into play in the bureaucratic environment of public or nonprofit ownership.

Far from being more cost-effective than private housing, subsidized housing is even more expensive than it first appears. Its cost includes the vast amount of property-tax revenue forgone when rental housing is held by public authorities or nontaxpaying nonprofit groups. By choosing to invest in housing, cities choose not to invest in other services, or not to leave money in the private economy to finance growth that would provide opportunity for poor and nonpoor alike. Under the Rebuild New York program championed by the Koch and Dinkins administrations, the city "invested" an estimated $5 billion (much of it from its own operating budget) in housing renovation and gave up millions in property-tax revenues by deeding buildings to nonprofit organizations.

The rejoinder, then, to the myth of the public or nonprofit alternative is that gleaming new projects are bound to decay—and to have significant long-term public costs. But for housing advocates, this is really just a political problem: that of making clear to the body politic that perpetually escalating subsidies to guarantee a safe and sanitary environment for the poor are the cost of living in a moral body politic. Here we arrive at the nub of their mistaken ideology.

Myth No. 3: *The moral qualities of the poor are a product of their housing "environment."* The essence of the housing advocates' worldview, as the New York Association for Improving the Condition of the Poor put it in 1854, is that "physical evils produce moral evils." Improved physical surroundings will lead people to become upright, ambitious, and successful. Perhaps the quintessential myth of environmental determinism is that kids who might otherwise have no place to do their homework have their own rooms in government-assisted housing—and therefore succeed where they would have failed.

There is much that is appealing in this view, which has a powerful hold on the liberal psyche. But the track record of public housing—which by almost any physical measure is superior to the housing in which most of its residents have previously lived—has hardly borne out the notion that better housing uplifts the poor. The response of housing reformers to drug- and gunfire-riddled projects has been not to reexamine the premise but to tinker with the model. Having long dwelled on design, they now devote equal attention to the social "environment." Thus Secretary Cisneros dreamed of new, low-rise, mixed-income subsidized housing that would correct the mistake of concentrating the poor in apartment towers now said to have encouraged crime. So, too, the nonprofit, "community-based" management of renovated apartment buildings is touted as a nurturing environment in which the poorest are inspired by gainfully employed "role-model" neighbors to improve their habits and their lot.

Here is where housing advocates most radically misunderstand the nature of the unsubsidized housing market. They can't see its crucial role in weaving a healthy social fabric and inspiring individuals to advance. By pushing to provide the poor with better housing than they could otherwise afford, housers are blind to the fact that they are interfering with a delicate system that rewards effort and achievement by giving people the chance to live in better homes in better neighborhoods. In this unsubsidized system, you earn your way to a better neighborhood. In fact, you must help to create and to maintain better neighborhoods by your own effort.

Housing subsidies—whether in the form of subsidized apartments or even vouchers that you can take to a landlord of your choice—turn this system on its head and undermine it, for housing subsidies do not reward achievement; they reward need. Those who strive and save are offered the same subsidized unit as those on public assistance; the provident and the improvident become indistinguishable. Those who work must live alongside those who do not. To believe that this is just is to believe that the poor are fundamentally undifferentiated—that they are all the same in being victims of an oppressive system. Those done the greatest injustice by such naiveté are the hardworking poor, who find to their horror that their new neighbor in a housing project is a drug dealer, or that the house next door has been rented, through a housing voucher, to a mother on welfare who does not supervise her children.

Subsidies deny the self-sacrificing, working poor the chance to put physical and social distance between themselves and the nonworking or anti-social poor. The *New York Times* cited the case of a hardworking woman who found herself in a bad neighborhood surrounded by gang violence as evidence of the need for increased housing subsidies, but more likely it demonstrates the opposite. By subsidizing troubled families, perhaps with criminal members, so that they can live in the same neighborhoods as those who hold modest but honest jobs, we expose the law-abiding to the disorder and violence of the undisciplined and the lawless, depriving them of the decent neighbor-hoods—decent in values if shabby in appearance—that their efforts should earn them. If we fail to allow the hard-working to distinguish themselves, by virtue of where they live, from those who do not share these traits, we devalue them. Even if we could somehow subsidize only the good citizens, the deserving poor, we would still do them a grave disservice, fostering the belief that they have moved to bet-ter homes in better neighborhoods by dint of largesse, not accomplishment—an entirely different psychology.

A neighborhood of good housing is not necessarily a good neighborhood. And a poor and shabby neighborhood is not necessarily a bad neighborhood. The terms on which residents have come to a place, as well as the extent to which they own property and have otherwise invested in the upkeep and safety of it, matter far more. It is worth re-calling the distinctions sociologist Herbert Gans made among different types of poor neighborhoods. "In most American cities," he wrote, "there are two major types of low-rent neighborhoods: the areas of first and second set-tlement for urban migrants; and the areas that attract the criminal, the mentally ill, the socially rejected, and those who have given up the attempt to cope with life. The for-mer kind of area, in which immigrants try to adapt to the urban milieu . . . , may be called an urban village. The sec-ond kind of area, populated largely by single men, patho-logical families, people in hiding from themselves or society, and individuals who provide the most disreputable of illegal-but-demanded services to the rest of the commu-nity, . . . might be called an *urban jungle.*"

Subsidized housing does not differentiate between these groups. In fact it seeks to address the problems of the lawless by mixing them in among the law-abiding and upwardly mobile, who are regarded almost as mere instruments for the salvation of the disorderly. Because it is based on the myth that the lawless are victims rather than victimizers, such a policy makes victims of those who would build an urban village by enmeshing them in an unsafe, disorganized neighborhood.

True, the new subsidized projects run by community groups, with the advice of such sophisticated organizations as the Local Initiatives Support Corporation and the Enterprise Foundation, do seek to screen tenants so as to keep bad actors out of mixed-income developments. But it defies imagination to think that such a process will be as effective as the screening that the market does. Indeed, in its analysis of such housing in New York, the New School found that though 6 percent of tenants were in arrears on their rent, the eviction rate was still zero.

By remaining focused on the myth that physical conditions are the single most important quality of housing, housers have misunderstood the dynamics of neighborhoods—not merely as places where people live but as communities of shared ideals. As a result, they have blindly based new policies on old mistakes. Consider, for instance, recent housing initiatives that aim to promote racial integration by placing low-income minority families in apartments in the suburbs. These policies are a recipe for racial resentment, which has in fact developed. Asking working-class whites to accept the welfare poor—who would inspire discomfort whether white or black—as neighbors is the worst way to address the race issue. The right way is to enforce housing nondiscrimination laws and thus allow the diffusion of upwardly mobile minority-group members into neighborhoods where, if they at first appear to be outsiders, it is only by virtue of race, not class.

A realistic housing policy would strive for a nonsubsidized world in which many different sorts of housing form a housing ladder. The lower rungs would be modest indeed—as modest as the single-room-occupancy hotels that sprang up in San Diego when that city allowed dwellings with less-than-full bathrooms and limited parking. By relaxing its code requirements, the city catalyzed construction of some 2,700 new SRO units for the working poor—day laborers, cabdrivers, fast-food employees. The SROs have formed a housing ladder all their own: lower-rent buildings may have no TV or phone, while lobby guards in the better buildings enforce more stringent guest policies.

A sensible housing policy would purge housing and building codes of unnecessary barriers to construction. The New York City Housing Partnership, for instance, would like to build new versions of old-fashioned Brooklyn row houses, but handicapped-access laws forbid basement apartments, which allow for a less expensive overall design. Requirements for cast-iron or copper pipes instead of less expensive plastic ones, or for excessive numbers of electric outlets, increase the cost of housing needlessly. Hugely expensive environmental cleanup requirements discourage developers from building low-cost (or any other kind of) housing on the many "brownfield" sites of inner cities. Policymakers should push for safe ways to "minimally rehab" older buildings, so that they're not priced out of the reach of the unsubsidized poor. City Homes, a Baltimore developer, has tried this on a small scale, with the cooperation of local and state authorities that have held renovation requirements to a minimum. Because of its low costs, City Homes doesn't need the federal rent subsidies on which most low-income housing complexes depend. City Homes rents only to the employed and has created blocks—inhabited by nurses, city sanitation workers, and the like—that are oases of safety and civility in the midst of bad neighborhoods.

Even with building codes that focus on basic safety issues and try not to raise prices, there will be people who can't afford anything we think should be built. In some cases this may be the result of poverty despite effort. In others it may be the result of bad life choices and the wrong values. For those in temporary emergency situations, we should provide shelters, basic arrangements that ensure no one must live on the street. For those whose lack of housing is really a symptom of larger problems—the alcoholic, the drug addict, the teenage mother who cannot afford her own household—we can look to institutional ways, such as group homes, to deliver the combination of shelter, guidance, and treatment they need.

What about the subsidized housing we already have, including New York's 180,000 units of public housing? Ideally it would be sold off. If that is impracticable—and it would be complicated given the public financing involved as well as the politics of the situation—it may make sense to consider a limit on the time any person can live in a subsidized unit, especially now that welfare has a time limit. Or housing authorities might charge higher rents for apartments in "better" projects, so as to create a kind of housing ladder.

In this new order we would understand that a large, variegated supply is the way to restrain housing costs. We would understand that modest housing is a stage that people pass through—and that, by trying to stamp it out, we threaten to short-circuit the process by which they improve themselves. It is superficially attractive to give the hardworking breadwinner a leg up, a housing subsidy, to help pay the bills and raise his or her children. But in practice, because subsidies are provided on the basis of need, not effort or accomplishment, such a policy threatens not to solve our social problems but to make them permanent.

[1997]

# TWO

....................................................

# How Public Housing Harms Cities

Most policy experts agree these days that big public housing projects are noxious environments for their tenants. What's less well understood is how noxious such projects are for the cities that surround them. Housing projects radiate dysfunction and social problems outward, damaging local businesses and neighborhood property values. They hurt cities by inhibiting or even preventing these run-down areas from coming back to life by attracting higher-income homesteaders and new business investment. Making matters worse, for decades cities have zoned whole areas to be public housing forever, shutting out in perpetuity the constant recycling of property that helps dynamic cities generate new wealth and opportunity for rich and poor alike.

Public housing spawns neighborhood social problems because it concentrates together welfare-dependent, single-parent families, whose fatherless children disproportionately turn out to be school dropouts, drug users, nonworkers, and criminals. These are not, of course, the families public housing originally aimed to serve. But as the U.S. economy boomed after World War II, the lower-middle-class working families for whom the projects had been built discovered that they could afford privately built homes in America's burgeoning suburbs, and by the 1960s they had completely abandoned public housing. Left behind were the poorest, most disorganized nonworking families, almost all of them headed by single women. Public housing then became a key component of the vast welfare-support network that gave young women their own income and apartment if they gave birth to illegitimate kids. As the fatherless children of these women grew up and went astray, many projects became lawless places, with gunfire a nightly occurrence and murder commonplace.

The crime and disorder didn't stay within the confines of the blighted projects, as residents in neighborhoods dominated by public housing know only too well. Joe Petrone, a longtime resident of Philadelphia's East Falls neighborhood, where his family owns a real-estate business, has watched the whole life cycle of America's experiment in subsidized housing play out on his doorstep. The now demolished East Falls housing project opened some forty years ago as housing for working families. "We'd celebrate people 'graduating' from the projects," Petrone recalls of neighbors in those days. "We viewed it as an up and out situation." But as nonworking residents replaced the working ones, explains Petrone, a director of real estate for the city of Philadelphia, kids from the project began menacing the long blocks of privately owned row houses on adjoining Calumet Street and the neighborhood shopping area along

Ridge Avenue. "You'd have bricks coming through windows on Calumet Street, thrown from high-rises," he says. "Ninety percent of the robberies involved a perp who would disappear into the project."

The disorder exacted a huge toll on the neighborhood's economic vitality, Petrone says. "It got to the point where you wouldn't sell a three-story house in the area for more than $600"—a house that had once taken a whole working-class lifetime to own free of debt and that represented a family's life savings.

Some might dismiss Petrone's grumbling as the intolerance of a white ethnic for minority newcomers in his once overwhelmingly Italian-American neighborhood. They'd be dead wrong. You'll hear exactly the same complaints from hardworking minority residents of project-dominated neighborhoods too. "When you have single parents, you have lots of unsupervised teenagers and lots of drugs and gangs," observes Laurena Torres, an Italian-Hispanic East Harlem real-estate agent and property owner, whose rental brownstones look out on the Robert Wagner Homes, a spine of projects looming over First Avenue. "It affects your everyday life—you have to avoid the projects just to get to the cleaners, the laundry, or the grocery," she says. "None of us goes into them, or crosses through them—even at one o'clock in the afternoon—as a short cut."

Fear of those who live in housing projects can drive neighbors who can afford it to move—another drain on urban vitality, since these are often the striving, upwardly mobile people who make neighborhoods flourish. Torres remembers a day three years ago when the valued tenants living in one of her apartments—"a professional couple," she says—moved out after finding blood splattered on their stoop from a drug dispute that had (quite literally) spilled over from the projects. "They got up that morning," recalls Torres, "and said, 'This is enough.'" It's her upwardly mobile minority tenants, says Torres, who complain most about the "undesirable element from the projects."

Earnest Gates, founder of Chicago's Near West Side Community Development Corporation, once would have pooh-poohed the worries of Torres's ambitious minority tenants. During the late 1980s he tried to transform the Near West Side, a respectable lower-middle-class neighborhood with a substantial number of black homeowners, into an all-black community where all social classes would live side by side. Gates's experiment in racial social engineering required keeping white gentrifiers out, and he decided to use what he calls "the stigma of public housing" to do it. In exchange for dropping his organization's opposition to the construction of a new basketball stadium in his neighborhood, Gates won from the city the right to develop some seventy-five vacant, city-owned lots in the area. Working with the Chicago Housing Authority, he proceeded to mix new, owner-occupied homes with buildings featuring new public housing units.

Gates's gambit kept out interloping whites, all right; but it also enraged law-abiding minority homeowners who didn't much care for their new publicly housed neighbors, some of whom had turned their subsidized residences into crack dens. Gates had hoped that the hardworking poor would move into his subsidized units. Instead, he says ruefully, "We got the bad players." Today the middle-aged Gates, whose demeanor remains that of a stern, subtly confrontational sixties black militant, admits that he made a serious mistake. "I have regrets," he says, "and a lot of the homeowners here are pissed off at me."

To understand more fully how much damage public housing can inflict on neighborhoods like the Near West Side, consider what can happen when it disappears from a troubled area of a city. After northern Philadelphia's bleak Richard Allen Homes met with the wrecking ball a few years ago, developer Lawrence Rust pounced, putting together a detailed development plan for the derelict area near the demolished project. Soon he was gutting and renovating previously vacant buildings, and selling to yuppie gentrifiers. "I took fifteen Dumpsters filled with trash out of here," Rust tells some prospective buyers of a three-story loft he is renovating—a twenty-something graphic designer and a singer, both from New York. He's selling the row house he restored next door for $225,000, on a block where a few years ago houses went for $1,500, and property taxes were negligible.

The prospect of this kind of urban improvement has led Mayor Edward Lambert of Fall River, Massachusetts—a formerly depressed New England mill town starting to revive as a home for high-tech manufacturing and for Boston and Providence commuters—to push for the demolition of the hundred-unit Watuppa Heights housing project, despite a state offer to provide $6 million (or about $60,000 per apartment) to upgrade it. (State—and not, as is usually the case, federal—funds had originally bankrolled construction of the project.) He plans to replace the project with new owner-occupied homes, though developers may get city subsidies to keep the prices low.

Lambert, a Democrat, argued that Watuppa Heights

was a magnet, drawing households with social problems to his city from Boston and other cities with large numbers of residents eligible for subsidized housing. His office discovered that, out of seventeen hundred households waiting to receive public housing placement in Fall River, only two hundred actually lived in the city (and most of those had passed up available units in Watuppa Heights while waiting for apartments in newer, more desirable public housing). A *Boston Globe* article, reporting that Boston social workers were encouraging low-income households to move to the old mill town, where there was greater vacancy in the public housing system, provided further evidence that Watuppa was filling up with out-of-towners.

And they were disproportionately a bad lot. Statistics showed crime falling citywide but spiking in Watuppa Heights. New project residents coming from other cities, the mayor pointed out, brought with them "more police calls, more special-needs kids, more crime, and more drugs." As one mayoral aide noted, "The mayor wouldn't put it this way, but the basic argument was that you had people coming from all over to use our services and make the place trashy."

Perhaps surprisingly in a state where "affordable housing" is a mantra, the Massachusetts State Legislature recently gave Lambert the green light to demolish the project. The vote represented a big win for the mayor and for Fall River's state legislators—and a major turning point for a city fighting hard to improve its schools and its economy.

The destruction of a project like the Richard Allen Homes or Watuppa Heights, however, remains a relatively rare event. And this fact points to a second, more subtle way that public housing harms cities. Unlike privately

owned buildings, public housing becomes property permanently fixed in a particular, low-value use, even as cities
change and renew around it. Many projects have loomed
over their neighborhoods for decades now. The names of
some even suggest that the racial makeup of their residents
will always be the same: the two Borinquen Plazas in the
Bushwick section of Brooklyn seem forever intended for
Puerto Ricans, the Langston Hughes Apartments in Brooklyn's Brownsville neighborhood for African Americans, as if
some races are fated disproportionately to be poor, dysfunctional wards of the state—a mistaken and racist assumption that has characterized so much harmful social
policy over the last several decades. All the while, cities
never discover what new, imaginative uses the free market
might invent for these frozen areas.

In New York City the sheer quantity of property locked
into service as public housing works as a significant drag
on the city's economy. In East Harlem, where no fewer than
thirteen huge housing projects stand ("the world's greatest
concentration of public housing," city officials once
boasted), almost no part of the neighborhood escapes their
intimidating, prosperity-squelching presence. "We're surrounded on all sides by them—they're an eyesore, and
there's an awful lot of runoff, whether crime or drugs," says
one prominent property manager, whose firm owns thirteen hundred units in some sixty buildings in the area. "If
we had even half the number of projects," he laments,
"we'd be the next East Village, with our proximity to mid-
town and the Number 6 subway train going right through
the neighborhood."

But East Harlem isn't the only place in New York with
an excess of public housing. Gotham has vastly more pub-

lic housing units than any other city in the nation—nearly 200,000 of the national total of 1 million or so. (Chicago is a distant second, with 38,000 units.) Public housing occupies an astounding 2,500 acres of real estate in New York, the equivalent of 156 World Trade Center sites: a city within the city.

This profusion of public housing also reduces the space available for private housing—a real problem in a city where private housing, especially in the middle-income price range, is in perennially short supply. One New York neighborhood facing this problem is the Brooklyn Navy Yard area, home of a former shipbuilding operation that's now an industrial park, with 3,500 employees working for dozens of small businesses. Many more firms will probably join these companies once a planned new movie studio opens in the neighborhood. Yet there's virtually no housing available in the vicinity for the industrial park's middle-income workers, because two big public housing projects use up much of the area's space and discourage residential development in the rest. Says Richard Drucker of the Brooklyn Navy Yard Development Corporation, the non-profit that runs the yard under lease from the city, "There's a great demand for middle-income housing in the area. If you could build it, it would sell." And if such housing replaced the projects? Replies Drucker: "Brooklyn would be better off."

Nevertheless, the challenge of freeing the Brooklyn Navy Yard and other urban neighborhoods across the nation from public housing is daunting. The belief that "public housing ye shall always have with you" is sacrosanct among housing advocates and officials. Like public housing's originators more than a half-century ago, they are convinced that the private housing market will always exclude the poor, making public housing permanently essential.

It is this assumption that drives the Department of Housing and Urban Development's ongoing multi-billion-dollar Hope VI reform initiative, the latest in an endless series of HUD efforts to remedy the endless failures of its earlier housing programs. Hope VI has demolished seventy thousand aging public housing units nationwide (including Chicago's notorious Robert Taylor Homes), only to replace many of them with new units of a different design, in the belief that this time HUD will get the formula right.

As has been the fantasy of public housing officials from the beginning, HUD bureaucrats believe that the right kind of public housing can cure the ills of the "severely distressed." In this oft-disappointed belief, Hope VI is replacing many of the alienating high-rises it is tearing down with more comfy town houses, and it seeks to get higher-income families to move into the new units along with the very poor, thinking that the more successful families will set a good example for the less successful. "Hope VI will strike a balance and create stable communities," explains HUD Deputy Assistant Secretary Milan Ozdinec, a career bureaucrat in the agency. "It has the very low income side by side with the family earning 60 percent of median," he says. "That's where connections are made, examples are set, and social capital built."

But this is mere wishful thinking. Why assume that the poor and dysfunctional will learn from the more successful? Isn't it just as likely that the children of the dysfunctional will set a bad and potentially damaging example for the children of the successful? Did Earnest Gates's public housing tenants learn from the more prosperous blacks of Chicago's Near West Side? The burned-out crack houses suggest otherwise—as do the noisy, unkempt properties rented by federal housing-voucher tenants in respectable working-class neighborhoods nationwide. Moreover, it is far from certain that many Hope VI projects will be able to attract a mix of households in the first place. Why would those with the means to live elsewhere choose to move, say, into new Hope VI public housing going up in the badlands of Chicago's South Side?

Hope VI only perpetuates public housing's ill effect on cities. On the former site of the closed East Falls public housing project, the Philadelphia Housing Authority is building 304 new Hope VI units. In this new development, christened Schuylkill Falls, half the units will go to low-income tenants, even though the site borders Schoolhouse Lane, some of the most desirable real estate in the city. Real estate official Joe Petrone, part of a citizens' group seeking to block construction of the new units, says, "We live in fear right now of them duplicating what we had for forty years. They're just putting a tuxedo on a pig. It's still a pig." Petrone estimates that privately developed, unsubsidized condominiums built on the site could sell for $300,000 or $400,000 each—high for Philadelphia. "The tax ratables for the city would be tremendous," he adds. "God knows the city of Philadelphia needs them."

You'll hear similar complaints about lost opportunity in Chicago. A black candidate for alderman scoffs at plans to replace the Robert Taylor Homes with new mid-rises on the site. "What I'd really like to see there," says the candidate, "is an Ikea. The site is right off the expressway. It'd be perfect for retail."

Even in a Hope VI development widely regarded as successful—Chicago's North Town Village—missed opportunity abounds. North Town Village went up several years ago on what had been vacant land adjacent to the infamous Cabrini-Green project, and it provides the model for what is to come in Chicago's public housing system. The city required the developer to include a mix of income levels in the project. And here, at least for now, it has happened—no doubt because the land is in the heart of one of the hottest real estate markets in the city: nearby North Avenue, once derelict in the long shadow of dangerous Cabrini-Green, today pulsates with national chain stores and sparkling restaurants. But by mandating that 79 of North Town Village's 261 apartments rent to Housing Authority tenants, and that another 39 rent for below-market rates, the city has greatly diminished the prices of other units in the buildings and the property tax that the buildings generate. "We could be selling condos here for $800,000; instead we're selling them for $425,000," observes Peter Holsten, the developer—though he's not complaining, since public funding ensures steady profits for his company. "We're paying $2 million in taxes," he adds. "But it could easily be double that."

Not that such mundane considerations seem to matter to housing officials. HUD Deputy Assistant Secretary Ozdinec happily—even proudly—concedes that many public housing sites could support higher-end uses. He rattles off examples of Hope VI sites in recovering neighborhoods that private builders would snap up in a heartbeat if HUD would just let them. In Houston, he observes, land values around the demolished Allen Parkway Village "went up so fast, we had to scramble to put together enough land to build something else"—that is, public housing instead of higher-value private development. In San Francisco the North Beach Hope VI project borders the famed Fisherman's Wharf. "If something else had been built there," says Ozdinec, "it would have been a tremendous economic boon for the city of San Francisco." Under a Republican administration, such cavalier dismissal of urban prosperity, even by a career HUD official, is dispiriting.

If HUD officials, in their unimaginative bureaucratic way, can't conceive of life without public housing, "affordable housing activists" would view any effort to shrink the size of the public housing system or phase it out entirely as outrageous heresy to be opposed tooth and nail. In Fall River, for example, a legal services advocacy group, the Massachusetts Law Reform Institute, has pledged that it will try to block the demolition of Watuppa Heights "every step of the way," as the *Boston Globe* puts it. In Chicago the local housing authority faces constant pressure from tenant organizers such as the Community Renewal Society, a "social justice" organization that has pushed for one-to-one replacement of any public housing unit that the city happens to tear down plus a lifetime "right of return" for any tenant displaced by project demolitions.

Housing officials and angry activists notwithstanding, however, the truth is that any two-income working family can afford private housing in the United States. For example, the average rent for an apartment in New York City, excluding pricey Manhattan, is just $604. That means that for a two-income family at the minimum wage, fully 40 percent of the apartments in the outer boroughs would cost them no more than 30 percent of their income to rent. In New York, of course, the average *dishwasher* makes $2 or so above the minimum wage; nationwide, few workers, except for illegal aliens, stay at the minimum wage for long.

When housing advocates say that the private housing market will inevitably fail the poor, then, it's really low-income unmarried mothers and their children whom they have in mind. And it is true that many of these families pose real problems for anyone who proposes to do away with public housing. Anyone who had visited Chicago's Robert Taylor Homes before their demolition would have wondered whether many of its residents could ever establish their own financially independent households. It was a place of the rankest degradation, where the crumbling, graffiti-covered walls and urine-reeking stairwells signaled the breakdown of order and civility, where young men freely used drugs in the common areas, where thirty-eight-year-old mothers wheeled around twenty-two-year-old sons left crippled by drug-related shootings, where work and marriage were abstractions—and yet where many dependent tenants, inured to the misery surrounding them, never wanted to leave.

It would be a boon to cities if they could get rid of such misbegotten places. By incubating social pathology, and by keeping so much property permanently off the property-tax rolls, public housing has sapped urban vitality. Although affordable housing activists deny it with their last breath, the gentrification that public housing inhibits is a good thing for cities, the urban poor included. It provides the housing that growing, high-paying businesses need if they are to attract the highly skilled workers who are their lifeblood—and whose high wages provide economic opportunity for so many other workers at all income levels. It is this economic dynamism that creates the opportunity city, in which there is a job for everyone and no one has to depend on government for his income or his housing.

How then might we dismantle the public housing system without hurting its most fragile residents? Any attempt to do so would have to be gradual, especially in a place like New York, where subsidized housing is such a large part of the residential real estate system. Some housing projects would have to remain as de facto poorhouses for the most dysfunctional. But by placing time limits on new tenants entering public housing—as the city of Charlotte, North Carolina, has done (see Chapter Six)—it would be feasible to reduce the overall number of subsidized housing units steadily. Knowing that the promise of a lifetime of subsidized housing was gone (along with a lifetime of welfare payments since the 1996 reform), young single mothers would be less likely to enter the system—and perhaps less likely to have children out of wedlock in the first place. Some current tenants (the least dysfunctional) could be offered housing vouchers that they could use in the private housing market in exchange for vacating public housing. The voucher would come with a time limit too, to discourage dependency. As the number of tenants fell, it would then become possible to sell some public housing buildings (or at least the sites, after the demolition of the emptied buildings) to private buyers, bringing more property back onto the tax rolls.

This does not mean that government would have no role to play in the creation of affordable housing. A compassionate conservative housing policy would work to dismantle the myriad government-made obstacles to the creation of housing by the private market—such barriers to building as rent control, irrational zoning regulations, expensive permit requirements, and overly demanding building codes. With such obstacles removed, newly dynamic urban economies could then be free to create private housing for *all* income groups, as they did decades ago, in the days when Boston three-deckers, Chicago two-flats, Brooklyn brownstones, and Oakland bungalows housed so many millions of struggling working families on their way toward the middle class. Cities would be better places for it—at all income levels.

[2003]

# THREE

Let's End
Housing Vouchers

Although crime-ridden high-rise projects are
public housing policy's most abiding symbol, the majority
of today's subsidized tenants don't live in them. Instead 1.7
million households now get government vouchers that help
pay their rent in the private market, at a cost of more than
$13 billion a year—a third of HUD's total budget. Liberals
embrace these vouchers because they believe poor families
can never afford decent market-rate housing; conservatives
like the vouchers' ostensible free-market mechanism,
which harnesses the private sector to serve a public goal. In
Washington the only question is how much to increase
spending on the program. But out in the blue-collar and
middle-class neighborhoods where voucher holders in-
creasingly live, longtime residents hate the program. It undermines and destabilizes their communities by importing
social problems into their midst, they say—vociferously
enough to get the attention of local legislators. Although

the program's supporters dismiss the critics (some of whom are black) as racists, they are nothing of the kind. And they are right.

In south suburban Chicago, with one of the highest concentrations of voucher holders in the country, middle-class African-American residents complain that they thought they'd left the ghetto behind—only to find that the federal government is subsidizing it to follow them. Vikkey Perez of Richton Park, Illinois, owner of Nubian Beauty Supply, fears that the small signs of disorder that have come with voucher tenants—the unmowed lawns and shopping carts left in the street—could undermine the neighborhood. "Their lifestyle," she says, "doesn't blend with our suburban lifestyle." Kevin Moore, a hospital administrator and homeowner in nearby Hazelcrest, complains that children in voucher homes go unsupervised. Boom boxes play late at night. "I felt like I was back on the West Side," he says, referring to the Chicago ghetto where he grew up. "You have to remember how to act tough."

In South Philadelphia's Irish and Italian neighborhoods, which have seen an influx of voucher holders, elected officials report being inundated with constituent complaints—and watching white constituents move out of the neighborhood. The area's state representative, William Keller, describes how owners of row houses suddenly find that "the house next door is being rented to people whose kids are up all night, who are out in the street yelling 'M-F' this and 'M-F' that. It's like they're trying to find the worst people." The issue, he says, "isn't race; it's class."

In Maryland's Prince George's County, an area of the Washington, D.C., suburbs with a large concentration of middle-class black residents, hundreds of voucher tenants—many of whom come from Washington, since vouchers are portable from one jurisdiction to another—do not pay their utility bills or their required 30 percent share of the rent. "We're very concerned about the program," says Mary Lou McDonough of the Prince George's Housing Authority, which doles out the vouchers. The authority is concerned about more than nonpayment. Unlike most such agencies, it screens its voucher applicants, and it finds that some of the households have criminal records—including, recently, a murder conviction. Every year the authority boots out twenty-five or thirty voucher holders for brand-new crimes, usually drug related.

How could so politically popular a program become so fraught with trouble? The problem lies both in the program's underlying assumptions and its governing regulations. The idea began with Lyndon Johnson's Kaiser Commission on Urban Housing, which mistakenly believed that the private housing market couldn't provide the poor with decent homes they could afford, despite the fact that for much of the twentieth century it had done so quite well. "The root of the problem in housing America's poor," the commissioners wrote, "is the gap between the price that private enterprise must receive and the price the poor can afford. The economic gap separating millions of deprived families from adequate housing can only be bridged by government subsidies. Such subsidies create an effective and real market demand to which private enterprise has proved it will respond."

Accepting this rationale, the Nixon administration, stung by scandals and cost overruns in federally subsidized housing construction, proposed the Housing and Community Development Act of 1974, whose Section 8 authorized federal rent subsidies for privately owned apartments. These so-called Section 8 vouchers appealed to Republicans because of their contrast with public housing built and operated at government expense. Not only did vouchers rely on the private market, they did not require public housing's ongoing maintenance costs.

As the program expanded, Republican officials continued to focus on the mechanics and efficiency of the program, without stopping to reconsider its fundamental assumption that, without subsidies, the private housing market couldn't serve the poor. For example, John Weicher, a HUD deputy assistant secretary, maintained that, through Section 8, "we can achieve the modest degree of improvement needed to bring many of our dwellings up to current quality standards and can provide significant financial relief for many hard-pressed poor families." The program, he thought, would allow the poor to move to "better neighborhoods," as if—another faulty assumption—a move to a middle-class environment would make them middle class.

Today's housing bureaucrats continue to take as gospel the Kaiser Commission's core belief that housing—unless it's a shanty or a cold-water flat—will inevitably be too expensive for families of modest means. One example of many: an HUD press release in March 2000 bore the headline GOOD TIMES FOR MANY DON'T END HARD TIMES FOR LOW-INCOME RENTERS; DESPITE ECONOMIC BOOM, HUD FINDS HOUSING CRISIS DEEPENING.

But federal numbers don't support this assertion. Poor families *can* afford existing private housing without a subsidy—as long as the family has two earners. The federal government figures that a family of four in Philadelphia needs $27,000 to afford a house—that's where the voucher kicks in. But this is only barely above the $24,000 that two people earning the minimum wage would jointly earn. The additional support the Earned Income Tax Credit gives the working poor would close this "housing gap" even further, providing a $1,300 payment to a household with two children. In other words, the government officially presumes that a household in which two people earn only barely more than the minimum wage (and in a time of full employment, many unskilled workers make more) could afford private, unsubsidized housing. (Of course, a stay-at-home spouse who saved a family child-care expenses would have the same economic effect as a second job holder.) Our "housing problem," then, really is just another name for our single-parent family and illegitimacy problems, with female-headed households making up more than 80 percent of voucher holders (and a comparable percentage of public housing tenants too).

Erroneous assumptions about housing affordability rest upon a failure to understand the importance of the means—marriage and thrift, above all—by which families improve their prospects so they can move to a good home in a good neighborhood. Better neighborhoods are not better because of something in the water but because people have built and sustained them by their efforts, their values, and their commitments. Voucher appropriations are based not only on the mistaken belief that it is necessary to award, at public expense, a better home to all who can demonstrate "need," but also that it is uplifting to do so, when in fact it is the effort to achieve the good home, rather than the good home in itself, that is the real engine of uplift.

Add to these misunderstandings the unanticipated effects of the Section 8 program's design, and you have a lethal mix. Although anyone earning less than 80 percent of the median income in theory qualifies for the program, vouchers are in limited supply, and priority goes to the poorest applicants. By law, fully 75 percent of vouchers must go to households earning only 30 percent or less of median family income. Local housing authorities can go even further in targeting the "neediest"; a quarter of Philadelphia's vouchers, for instance, go to those living in homeless shelters. These priorities are what torque the voucher program toward single-parent households, the country's lowest income group.

The priority given to such households, many of them on welfare or only recently off the rolls, forms part of a package of benefits—including food stamps, Medicaid, and the Earned Income Tax Credit—that have no time limits and that, taken together, constitute significant continuing public support for single-parent low-income households. So counter does this open-ended housing voucher run to welfare reform's five-year limit that Philadelphia's brochures describing the program stress that, no, there really is no time limit.

What's more, the program has the effect of concentrating problem-ridden, very poor single-parent families in specific neighborhoods. Under normal circumstances, Section 8 tenants would be concentrated anyway. Most landlords would shun them, for fear they would damage their property. Only owners of hard-to-rent, run-down buildings would welcome them, and these properties would be concentrated in marginal neighborhoods struggling hard to maintain their respectability. Other things being equal, landlords would try hard to find respectable working-class tenants before renting to subsidized Section 8 families.

But other things are not equal. Voucher tenants come with significant advantages to outweigh their drawbacks. Landlords don't have to worry about nonpayment, since the government deposits its share of the rent—the lion's share—directly into the property owner's bank account. Moreover, for properties in precariously respectable neighborhoods, the government-paid rent is more than the market rent. Reason: the Section 8 program allows voucher holders to pay up to the average rent in their entire metropolitan area, and landlords in working-class or lower-middle-class neighborhoods, where rents are below average, simply charge voucher holders exactly that average rent. Assured payment and a more than generous risk premium: no wonder some landlords in neighborhoods teetering on the brink of respectability gladly welcome voucher tenants over working-class families looking for lower rents, and so accelerate neighborhood decline. South Philadelphia state representative William Keller tells of local property owners who "couldn't rent their place for $500, but they can get $900 from Section 8."

The result is a familiar government-subsidized racket: landlords who specialize in Section 8s—who advertise for them and know the bureaucratic rules about what it takes to get paid. In Philadelphia, state representatives and members of the city council say they get daily complaints about Section 8 tenants, and they keep a list of landlords and their Section 8 holdings. "There are guys with 100 Section 8 houses," says Philadelphia city councilman James Kenney. "They're clearing $40,000 a month just in Section 8 income." In south suburban Chicago, Section 8 tenants have taken over whole subdivisions of attached row houses. One subdivision in the Riverdale suburb is now a virtual Section 8 ghetto, with more than 200 voucher holders, and the whole of Riverdale has 336 voucher households out of a total population of just 13,000. Locals have nicknamed the bus that takes many of these minority voucher holders to the plentiful low-wage jobs of the western suburbs the "Apartheid Express."

As Democratic Senator Barbara Mikulski of Maryland points out, vouchers are replacing "vertical ghettos with horizontal ones." An HUD study of "housing voucher location patterns" has found that in eleven of the nation's fifty largest cities there is at least one neighborhood where voucher holders constitute 25 percent of all households. The southern suburbs of Chicago, where anger over Section 8 is reaching the boiling point, have absorbed almost 58 percent of all the Cook County Housing Authority's vouchers—more, in other words, than all the other parts of Chicago and its suburbs combined. All but a handful of the voucher holders who moved from Washington, D.C., to its suburbs ended up in Maryland's Prince George's County. In Philadelphia, 45 percent of voucher holders inhabit just two of the city's five major sections—South Philadelphia and Northeast Philadelphia—blue-collar areas unaccustomed to subsidized housing. These are typical, not isolated, examples.

The effects of a concentration of voucher holders on a small municipality are profound. "It has touched every aspect of the city government," says Riverdale mayor Joe Szabo. Like most of the municipalities south of Chicago, where the now-vanished steel mills and other heavy industry once clustered, this town of small ranch houses dwarfed by looming power-line stanchions has always been a solidly blue-collar place, with an active community life. Recently, though, Szabo has noticed things changing. There are more children than ever in town, but the once popular youth football program has died. "We just can't get parent volunteers," he says. The mayor pushes park officials to mount more and more programs for lower-income children but finds that the kids' mothers just don't take the time to sign them up. "We'd have to go to individual households and convince them to send their kids, and even then they might not show up," he reports.

Demands have risen, though, for other sorts of public services. EMT crews respond to emergency calls to find callers, accustomed to city emergency rooms, simply saying they're "feeling ill." Riverdale's Potter Elementary School, which once boasted a top academic reputation, now has the state's highest student turnover. Student achievement has dropped—putting paid to the idea that shipping poor families to good schools in the suburbs will cause an education ethic to rub off. Instead the concentration of disorganized families has undermined a once good school. School funds, says the mayor, must now be diverted to the legions of "special needs" students. Crime is up too— "we have real legitimate gang issues now," the mayor says—and the city has had to increase its police force by 35 percent, from twenty-six to thirty-five. That's pushing the tax rate up, which the mayor fears will discourage new home buyers, driving the small city into a cycle of decline. A lack of local buying power—a function of the voucher program's preference for very low-income renters—has already left storefronts abandoned on Riverdale's main street.

Wayne Curry, the elected county executive of Maryland's Prince George's County (and the first African American to hold the job), has similar worries about the impact of voucher holders on his jurisdiction. As the *Washington Post* observed: "Curry is trying to grow the economic base of Prince George's—which has one of the nation's largest black middle-class communities—by attracting higher-income residents that draw merchants and businesses. Taking in a larger share of the region's poor runs counter to that goal."

Vouchers can lead to the deterioration of individual properties as well as of whole neighborhoods. Most landlords are unwilling to rent to voucher tenants: 40 percent of the voucher funds in Cook County, and $1 billion nationally, went unused because voucher holders couldn't find landlords willing to accept their scrip. Throughout California, where landlords can find solid working-class tenants who can pay more than the vouchers pay, voucher tenants are not welcome. So voucher holders, once they succeed in finding housing, tend not to rock the boat, contrary to the expectation that they would exert leverage on landlords to keep up their properties. Moreover, observes assistant manager Patrick Finn of the village of Flossmoor in south suburban Chicago, "If you are only paying $200, and you're getting a $700 or $800 apartment, your expectations are low. It's not your money. Section 8 supports the weakest section of the real-estate market—the house that can't sell, the absentee owner who doesn't perform well in the private marketplace. It subsidizes the marginal sector."

Although in theory the voucher program was supposed to promote racial integration as inner-city minority households used their vouchers to move to previously all-white suburban neighborhoods, the effect in practice appears to be just the opposite. Vouchers are creating new all-black communities. Joe Martin, director of an organization that has been trying for more than twenty years to attract middle-class African-American newcomers to south suburban Chicago while retaining long-term white residents, notes that the spread of voucher holders makes his already difficult task harder. "Voucher holders," he says, "have the effect of confirming the worst stereotypes." Racial integration is hard enough when whites and blacks are at relatively similar incomes. Mixing poverty-level blacks—by design of the Section 8 program—with middle-class whites is a recipe for racial instability.

But voucher-related racial problems are not confined to suburbs. The majority of voucher placements are, in fact, in lower-income urban neighborhoods, many of which are oases of hardworking families trying to maintain their properties. These are people who must be allowed to distinguish themselves from the disorderly poor. When the shabby-genteel neighborhood is white and the disorderly poor who arrive are black, the mixture is explosive—as in Philadelphia, where the Housing Authority has consistently placed the "worst stereotypes," minority former shelter residents and long-term public housing tenants, in historically white ethnic blue-collar neighborhoods.

In South Philly the neighborhood office of state representative William Keller bustles with irate residents whose entire net worth is tied up in their homes and who fear that the presence of voucher holders will undermine the value of their property. At a city council hearing in 1999, Lynne Rototli of the Mayfair Civic Association in Northeast Philly blamed vouchers for the fact that property values in her neighborhood were declining while taxes were going up. Residents of absentee-owned rental properties did not participate in community life, she said, and subsidized tenants kept late hours, making it hard for those getting up to go to work in the morning to sleep. "We are afraid," she told the council hearing, "that the Section embodies everything that we, the middle-class people, fear."

One tragedy in the voucher saga is that some black elected officials—Pennsylvania congressman Chaka Fattah, for instance—dismiss such heartfelt concerns as racist. Such attacks leave bitterness in their wake. "You know what bothers me?" one South Philadelphia resident confided in Representative Keller's office. "I've got two kids. You know why I don't have three? Because I can't afford it. And I see people with three or four kids and no father getting a subsidy to live in my neighborhood—which means I'm paying to help them. And complaining about it makes me a racist." Being black doesn't shield you from being labeled with the R-word when you attack Section 8. African-American local officials in predominantly black Matteson, Illinois, report that they've been accused of racism over the city's decision to advise landlords that it may be better to leave a unit temporarily vacant than to rent to a voucher holder.

Harvard sociologist William Julius Wilson famously argued that class, not race, is the most powerful divide that separates Americans today. Frank Arceneaux, an African-American state trooper who owns a home in Matteson and rental property in nearby Richton Park, illustrates Wilson's point as well as anyone—and he puts the lie to the idea that opposition to vouchers is inherently racist. He's become afraid to send his wife to collect rents in the apartment building he owns because of the presence of Section 8 tenants at a building nearby. "Section 8 brings a lifestyle from the city that I tried to escape from," he says. "It's a value difference. It's all single mothers. They let their kids stay out until midnight. I admit I'm prejudiced against blacks— blacks who don't honor my values. I can understand white flight. I'd like to fly too, but I can't. I've maxed out my income. I'm not gonna get rich all of a sudden. I've got to stay and fight."

Critics of the voucher program propose three fixes, all of dubious efficacy. The first is the idea of "deconcentrating" voucher holders. South suburban Chicago congressman Jerry Weller (who represents Riverdale) went so far as to propose a 20 percent cap on voucher holders in a given census tract. Congressman Jesse Jackson, Jr., who holds a key seat on the House Housing Committee, endorsed a version of the idea of a cap, or moratorium, in a letter to the *Chicago Sun-Times*. In a bid to placate his important constituency in the southern suburbs, Jackson proposed that the moratorium apply to any "South Side neighborhood or southern suburb that is experiencing zero or negative economic growth." But to spread out Section 8 tenants into other, wealthier neighborhoods would require HUD to pay even higher reimbursements to landlords—a tough sell to many legislators—and even so, landlords with other prospective tenants to choose from would resist voucher holders. It is so difficult to place voucher tenants in so-called nontraditional areas that a south suburban Chicago nonprofit dedicated to that purpose—Housing Choice Partners—has been able to place only 225 of 9,200 voucher holders outside the Section 8 corridors, despite personal counseling of voucher holders and assurance to landlords that the prospective tenants were not disruptive.

A second proposed improvement, also aimed at deconcentrating voucher tenants, is to align the value of vouchers more closely with actual private rents in a given neighborhood, to make the program less of a windfall for the owners of marginal housing. But for landlords willing to amass large blocks of such properties to rent to Section 8 tenants, the guarantee of even average rents in poor neighborhoods, deposited directly into their bank accounts each month by the government, will remain a temptation. It's an easy, risk-free way to make money.

The last proposed fix is to screen tenants. In fact housing authorities already have legislative license to screen out those who haven't paid their rent in the past or who have criminal convictions, but they are reluctant to do so. Observes a senior HUD official closely familiar with the Section 8 program: "If a family's been evicted for disturbance—drinking, making noise—typically the authority won't screen those families out. Authorities tend not to like to do heavy screening, because it puts them in a position of having to justify their actions legally. They're worried about some Legal Aid lawyer who's going to rake over their files and make their lives miserable." And if screening is difficult, revoking vouchers after a renter has moved in requires a major effort on the part of housing authorities. While housing authorities should certainly try to improve screening and should deal firmly with rowdy tenants, such screening cannot easily replace the screening that the housing market, left alone, would do to protect and sustain neighborhoods.

But maybe we would do better to rethink this issue completely. We could house the same population we now house with vouchers—primarily single mothers—in existing public housing projects. But we could transform those projects into something very different from what they are now—into institutional homes where unwed mothers could stay only for a fixed period of time (perhaps two years), during which time they might get instruction in parenting along with encouragement to marry the fathers of their children. Such a system envisions personal and cultural change, not just redistribution of income. In this respect, even no system at all would be better than Section 8 vouchers. Were the public to withdraw the support that enables single-parent families to get their own apartments, the women might be forced to consider marriage or to live with their own extended families, which might provide more supervision for the children. As matters stand now, a young woman who has children as a teenager can qualify, at age eighteen, for her own voucher-paid house, and she can keep it in perpetuity. If her income is low because she has no work experience, she would get top priority.

Even if we were to accept the dubious Johnson administration view that the poor need more income in order to afford better housing, that doesn't mean that rent vouchers would be the right way to provide it. Through the Earned Income Tax Credit, poor working families today can qualify for tax "refunds" larger than the amount actually withheld from their paychecks. If we're convinced that we must provide financial support to the working poor, far better to do it this way—or to reduce the regressive Social Security tax—than to provide housing vouchers. Even with such an income supplement, a household would still have to strive and save to find a home in a better neighborhood. Its relationship with a landlord would not be distorted. It would have to adopt the habits of thrift and discipline that would win favor with middle-class neighbors.

What our experience with Section 8 vouchers teaches us is simply this: replacing an old failure with a new one should not be confused with success.

[2000]

. . . . . . . . . . . . . . . . . . . . . . . . . . . . . . . . . . . . . . . . . . . . . . . . . .

# FOUR

# The Trillion-Dollar Bank Shakedown That Bodes Ill for Cities

The Clinton administration turned the Community Reinvestment Act, a once obscure and lightly enforced banking regulation law, into one of the most powerful mandates shaping American cities—and, as former Senate Banking Committee chairman Phil Gramm memorably put it, a vast extortion scheme against the nation's banks. Under its provisions, U.S. banks have committed nearly $1 trillion for inner-city and low-income mortgages and real-estate development projects, most of it funneled through a nationwide network of left-wing community groups intent, in some cases, on teaching their low-income clients that the financial system is their enemy and, implicitly, that government, rather than their own striving, is the key to their well-being.

The CRA's premise sounds unassailable: helping the poor buy and keep homes will stabilize and rebuild city neighborhoods. As enforced today, though, the law portends just the opposite, threatening to undermine the efforts of the upwardly mobile poor by saddling them with neighbors who are more than usually likely to depress property values by not maintaining their homes adequately or by losing them to foreclosure. The CRA's logic also helps to ensure that inner-city neighborhoods stay poor by discouraging the kinds of investments that might make them better off.

The act, which Jimmy Carter signed in 1977, grew out of the complaint that urban banks were "redlining" inner-city neighborhoods, refusing to lend to their residents while using their deposits to finance suburban expansion. The CRA decreed that banks have "an affirmative obligation" to meet the credit needs of the communities in which they are chartered, and that federal banking regulators should assess how well they do that when considering their requests to merge or to open branches. Implicit in the bill's rationale was a belief that the CRA was needed to counter racial discrimination in lending, an assumption that later seemed to gain support from a widely publicized 1990 Federal Reserve Bank of Boston finding that blacks and Hispanics suffered higher mortgage-denial rates than whites, even at similar income levels.

In addition, the act's backers claimed, the CRA would be profitable for banks. They just needed a push from the law to learn how to identify profitable inner-city lending opportunities. Going one step further, the Treasury Department recently asserted that banks that *do* figure out ways to reach inner-city borrowers might not be able to stop competitors from using similar methods—and therefore would not undertake such marketing in the first place without a push from Washington.

None of these justifications holds up, however, because of the changes that reshaped America's banking industry in the 1990s. Banking in the 1970s, when the CRA was passed, was a highly regulated industry in which small, local savings banks, rather than commercial banks, provided most home mortgages. Regulation prohibited savings banks from branching across state lines and sometimes even limited branching within states, inhibiting competition, the most powerful defense against discrimination. With such regulatory protection, savings banks could make a comfortable profit without doing the hard work of finding out which inner-city neighborhoods and borrowers were good risks and which were not. Savings banks also had reason to worry that if they charged inner-city borrowers a higher rate of interest to balance the additional risk of such lending, they might jeopardize the protection from competition they enjoyed. Thanks to these artificially created conditions, some redlining of creditworthy borrowers doubtless occurred.

The insular world of the savings banks collapsed in the early nineties, however, the moment it was exposed to competition. Banking today is a far more wide-open industry, with banks offering mortgages through the Internet, where they compete hotly with aggressive on-line mortgage companies. Standardized, computer-based scoring systems now rate the creditworthiness of applicants, and the giant, government-chartered Fannie Mae and Freddie Mac have helped create huge pools of credit by purchasing mortgage loans and packaging large numbers of them together into securities for sale to bond buyers. With such intense competition for profits and so much money available to lend, it's hard to imagine that banks couldn't instantly figure out how to market to minorities or would resist such efforts for fear of inspiring imitators. Nor has the race discrimination argument for the CRA held up. A September 1999 study by Freddie Mac, for instance, confirmed what previous Federal Reserve and Federal Deposit Insurance Corporation studies had found: that African Americans have disproportionate levels of credit problems, which explains why they have a harder time qualifying for mortgage money. As Freddie Mac found, blacks with incomes of $65,000 to $75,000 a year have on average worse credit records than whites making under $25,000.

The Federal Reserve Bank of Dallas had it right when it said—in a paper pointedly entitled "Red Lining or Red Herring?"—"the CRA may not be needed in today's financial environment to ensure all segments of our economy enjoy access to credit." True, some households—those with a history of credit problems, for instance, or those buying homes in neighborhoods where reselling them might be difficult—may not qualify for loans at all, and some may have to pay higher interest rates in reflection of higher risk. But higher rates in such situations are balanced by lower house prices. This is not a conspiracy against the poor; it's how markets measure risk and work to make credit available.

Nevertheless, until recently the CRA didn't matter all that much. During the seventies and eighties, CRA enforcement was perfunctory. Regulators asked banks to demonstrate that they were trying to reach their entire "assessment area" by advertising in minority-oriented newspapers or by sending their executives to serve on the boards of local community groups. The Clinton administration changed this state of affairs dramatically. Ignoring the sweeping transformation of the banking industry since the CRA was passed, the Clinton Treasury Department's 1995 regulations made getting a satisfactory CRA rating much harder. The new regulations deemphasized subjective assessment measures in favor of strictly numerical ones. Bank examiners would use federal home-loan data, broken down by neighborhood, income group, and race, to rate banks on performance. There would be no more As for effort. Only results—specific loans, specific levels of service—would count. Where and to whom have home loans been made? Have banks invested in all neighborhoods within their assessment area? Do they operate branches in those neighborhoods?

Crucially, the new CRA regulations also instructed bank examiners to take into account how well banks responded to complaints. The old CRA evaluation process had allowed advocacy groups a chance to express their views on individual banks, and publicly available data on the lending patterns of individual banks allowed activist groups to target institutions considered vulnerable to protest. But for advocacy groups that were in the complaint business, the Clinton administration regulations offered a formal invitation. The National Community Reinvestment Coalition—a foundation-funded umbrella group for community activist groups that profit from the CRA—issued a clarion call to its members in a leaflet entitled "The New CRA Regulations: How Community Groups Can Get Involved." "Timely comments," the NCRC observed with a certain understatement, "can have a strong influence on a bank's CRA rating."

The Clinton administration's get-tough regulatory regime mattered so crucially because bank deregulation had set off a wave of mega-mergers, including the acquisition of the Bank of America by NationsBank, BankBoston by Fleet Financial, and Bankers Trust by Deutsche Bank. Regulatory approval of such mergers depended, in part, on positive CRA ratings. "To avoid the possibility of a denied or delayed application," advises the NCRC in its deadpan tone, "lending institutions have an incentive to make formal agreements with community organizations." By intervening—even just *threatening* to intervene—in the CRA review process, left-wing nonprofit groups have been able to gain control over eye-popping pools of bank capital, which they in turn parcel out to individual low-income mortgage seekers. A radical group called ACORN Housing has a $760 million commitment from the Bank of New York; the Boston-based Neighborhood Assistance Corporation of America has a $3 billion agreement with the Bank of America; a coalition of groups headed by New Jersey Citizen Action has a five-year, $13 billion agreement with First Union Corporation. Similar deals operate in almost every major U.S. city. Observes Tom Callahan, executive director of the Massachusetts Affordable Housing Alliance, which has $220 million in bank mortgage money to parcel out, "CRA is the backbone of everything we do."

In addition to providing the nonprofits with mortgage money to disburse, the CRA allows those organizations to collect a fee from the banks for their services in marketing the loans. The Senate Banking Committee has estimated that, as a result of the CRA, $9.5 billion so far has gone to pay for services and salaries of the nonprofit groups involved. To deal with such groups and to produce CRA compliance data for regulators, banks routinely establish separate CRA departments. A CRA consultant industry has sprung up to assist them. New financial services firms offer to help banks that think they have a CRA problem make quick "investments" in packaged portfolios of CRA loans to get into compliance.

The result of all this activity, argues the CEO of one midsize bank, is that "banks are promising to make loans they would have made anyway, with some extra aggressiveness on risky mortgages thrown in." Many bankers—and even some CRA advocates—share his view. As one Fed economist puts it, the assertion that the CRA was needed to force banks to see profitable lending opportunities is "like saying you need the rooster to tell the sun to come up. It was going to happen anyway." And indeed, a survey of the lending policies of Chicago-area mortgage companies by a CRA-connected community group, the Woodstock Institute, found "a tendency to lend in a wide variety of neighborhoods"—even though the CRA doesn't apply to such lenders.

If loans that win banks good CRA ratings were going to be made anyway, and if most of those loans are profitable, should the CRA, even if redundant, bother anyone? Yes: because the CRA funnels billions of investment dollars through groups that understand protest and political advocacy but not marketing or finance. This amateur delivery system for investment capital already shows signs that it may be going about its business unwisely. And a quiet change in the CRA's mission—so that it no longer directs credit only to specific *places*, as Congress mandated, but also to low- and moderate-income home buyers, wherever they buy their property—greatly extends the area where these groups can cause damage.

There is no more important player in the CRA-inspired mortgage industry than the Boston-based Neighborhood Assistance Corporation of America. Chief executive Bruce Marks has set out to become the Wal-Mart of home mortgages for lower-income households. Using churches and radio advertising to reach borrowers, he has made NACA a brand name nationwide, with offices in twenty-one states, and he plans to double that number within a year. With "delegated underwriting authority" from the banks, NACA itself—not the banks—determines whether a mortgage applicant is qualified, and it closes sales right in its own offices. It expects to close five thousand mortgages next year, earning a $2,000 origination fee on each. Its annual budget exceeds $10 million.

Marks, a Scarsdale native, New York University M.B.A., and former Federal Reserve employee, unabashedly calls himself a "bank terrorist"—his public relations spokesman laughingly refers to him as "the shark, the predator," and the NACA newspaper is named the *Avenger*. They're not kidding: bankers so fear the tactically brilliant Marks for his ability to disrupt annual meetings and even target bank executives' homes that they often call him to make deals before they announce any plans that will put them in the CRA's crosshairs. A $3 billion loan commitment by Nations-Bank, for instance, well in advance of its announced merger with Bank of America, "was a preventive strike," says one NACA spokesman.

Marks is unhesitatingly candid about his intent to use NACA to promote an activist, left-wing political agenda.

NACA loan applicants must attend a workshop that cele-brates—to the accompaniment of gospel music—the protests that have helped the group win its bank lending agreements. If applicants do buy a home through NACA, they must pledge to assist the organization in five "actions" annually—anything from making phone calls to full-scale "mobilizations" against target banks, "mau-mauing" them, as sixties' radicals used to call it. "NACA believes in aggres-sive grassroots advocacy," says its *Homebuyer's Workbook*.

The NACA policy agenda embraces the whole universe of financial institutions. It advocates tough federal usury laws, restrictions on the information that banks can pro-vide to credit-rating services, financial sanctions against banks with poor CRA ratings even if they're not about to merge or branch, and the extension of CRA requirements to insurance companies and other financial institutions. But Marks's political agenda reaches far beyond finance. He wants, he says, to do whatever he can to ensure that "working people have good jobs at good wages." The home mortgage business is his tool for political organizing: the *Homebuyer's Workbook* contains a voter registration appli-cation and states that "NACA's mission of neighborhood stabilization is based on participation in the political process. To participate you must register to vote." Marks plans to install a high-capacity phone system that can for-ward hundreds of calls to congressional offices—"or Phil Gramm's house"—to buttress NACA campaigns. The com-bination of an army of "volunteers" and a voter registration drive portends (though there is no evidence of this so far) that someday CRA-related funds and Marks's troop of CRA borrowers might end up fueling a host of Democratic can-didacies. During the Reagan years, the right used to talk of cutting off the flow of federal funds to left-liberal groups, a goal called "defunding the left"; through the CRA the Clinton administration has found a highly effective way of doing exactly the opposite, funneling millions to NACA or to outfits like ACORN, which advocates a nationalized health-care system, "people before profits at the utilities," and a tax code based "solely on the ability to pay."

Whatever his long-term political goals, Marks may well reshape urban and suburban neighborhoods because of the terms on which NACA qualifies prospective home buyers. While most CRA-supported borrowers would doubtless find loans in today's competitive mortgage industry, a small percentage would not, and NACA welcomes such buyers with open arms. "Our job," says Marks, "is to push the envelope." Accordingly, he gladly lends to people with less than $3,000 in savings, or with checkered credit histories or significant debt. Many of his borrowers are single-parent heads of household. Such borrowers are, Marks believes, fundamentally oppressed and at permanent disadvantage, and therefore society must adjust its rules for them. Hence NACA's most crucial policy decision: it requires no down payments whatsoever from its borrowers. A down-payment requirement, based on concern as to whether a borrower can make payments, is—when applied to low-income minority buyers—"patronizing and almost racist," Marks says.

This policy—"America's best mortgage program for working people," NACA calls it—is an experiment with extraordinarily high risks. There is no surer way to destabilize a neighborhood than for its new generation of home buyers to lack the means to pay their mortgages—which is likely to be the case for a significant percentage of those granted a no-down-payment mortgage based on their low-income classification rather than their good credit history. Even if such buyers do not lose their homes, they are a group more likely to defer maintenance on their properties, creating the problems that lead to streets going bad and neighborhoods going downhill. Stable or increasing property values grow out of the efforts of many; one unpainted house, one sagging porch, one abandoned property is a threat to the work of dozens, because such signs of neglect discourage prospective buyers.

A no-down-payment policy reflects a belief that poor families should qualify for home ownership because they are poor, in contrast to the reality that some poor families are prepared to make the sacrifices necessary to own property, and some are not. Keeping their distance from those unable to save money is a crucial means by which upwardly mobile, self-sacrificing people establish and maintain the value of the homes they buy. If we empower those with bad habits, or those who have made bad decisions, to follow those with good habits to better neighborhoods—thanks to CRA's new emphasis on lending to low-income borrowers no matter where they buy their homes—those neighborhoods will not remain better for long.

Because many of the activists' big-money deals with the banks are so new, no one knows for sure exactly what neighborhoods the community groups are flooding with CRA-related mortgages and what effect they are having on those neighborhoods. But some suggestive early returns are available from Massachusetts, where CRA-related advocacy has flourished for more than a decade. A study for a consortium of banks and community groups found that during the 1990s home purchases financed by nonprofit lenders have overwhelmingly not been in the inner-city areas where redlining had been suspected. Instead 41 percent of all the loans went to the lower-middle-class neighborhoods of Hyde Park, Roslindale, and Dorchester Center/Codman Square—Boston's equivalent of New York's borough of Queens—and additional loans went to borrowers moving to the suburbs. In other words, CRA lending appears to be helping borrowers move out of inner-city neighborhoods into better-off areas. Similarly, not-yet-published data from the state-funded Massachusetts Housing Partnership show that many new Dorchester Center, Roslindale, and Hyde Park home buyers came from much poorer parts of the city, such as the Roxbury ghetto. Florence Higgins, a home-ownership counselor for the Massachusetts Affordable Housing Alliance, confirms the trend, noting that many buyers she counsels lived in subsidized rental apartments before buying their homes.

This CRA-facilitated migration makes the mortgage terms of groups like NACA particularly troubling. In a September 1999 story, the *Wall Street Journal* reported, based on a review of court documents by Boston real estate analyst John Anderson, that the Fleet Bank initiated foreclosure proceedings against 4 percent of loans made for Fleet by NACA in 1994 and 1995—a rate four times the industry average. Overextended buyers don't always get much help from their nonprofit intermediaries, either: Boston radio station WBUR reported in July 2000 that home buyers in danger of losing their homes had trouble getting their phone calls returned by the ACORN Housing group.

NACA frankly admits that it is willing to run these risks. It emphasizes the virtues of the counseling programs it offers (like all CRA groups) to prepare its typical buyer—"a hotel worker with an income of $25K and probably some past credit problems," says a NACA spokesman—and it operates what it calls a "neighborhood stabilization fund" on which buyers who fall behind on payments can draw. But Bruce Marks says that he would consider a low foreclosure rate to be a problem. "If we had a foreclosure rate of 1 percent, that would just prove we were skimming," he says. Accordingly, in mid-1999, 8.2 percent of the mortgages NACA had arranged with the Fleet Bank were delinquent, compared with the national average of 1.9 percent. "Considering our clientele," Marks asserts, "nine out of ten would have to be considered a success."

The no-down-payment policy has sparked so sharp a division within the CRA industry that the National Community Reinvestment Coalition has expelled Bruce Marks and NACA from its ranks over it. The precipitating incident: when James Johnson, then CEO of Fannie Mae, made a speech to NCRC members on the importance of down payments to keep mortgage-backed securities easily salable, NACA troops, in keeping with the group's style of personalizing disputes, distributed pictures of Johnson, captioned: "I make $6 million a year, and I can afford a down payment. Why can't you?" Says Josh Silver, research director of NCRC: "There is no quicker way to undermine CRA than through bad loans." NCRC represents hundreds of smallish community groups, many of which do insist on down payments—and many of which make loans in the same neighborhoods as NACA and understand the risk its philosophy poses. Still, whenever NACA opens a new branch office, it will be difficult for the nonprofits already operating in that area to avoid matching its come-one, come-all terms.

Even without a no-down-payment policy, the pressure

on banks to make CRA-related loans may be leading to foreclosures. Although bankers generally cheerlead for CRA out of fear of being branded racists if they do not, the CEO of one midsize bank grumbles that 20 percent of his institution's CRA-related mortgages, which required only $500 down payments, were delinquent in their very first year, and probably 7 percent will end in foreclosure. "The problem with CRA," says an executive with a major national financial services firm, "is that banks will simply throw money at things because they want that CRA rating." From the banks' point of view, CRA lending is simply a price of doing business—even if some of the mortgages must be written off. The growth in very large banks—ones most likely to sign major CRA agreements—also means that those advancing the funds for CRA loans are less likely to have to worry about the effects of those loans going bad: such loans will be a small portion of their lending portfolios.

Looking into the future gives further cause for concern: "The bulk of these loans," notes a Federal Reserve economist, "have been made during a period in which we have not experienced an economic downturn." The Neighborhood Assistance Corporation of America's own success stories make you wonder how much CRA-related carnage will result in a weak economy. The group likes to promote, for instance, the story of Renea Swain-Price, grateful for NACA's negotiating on her behalf with Fleet Bank to prevent foreclosure when she fell behind on a $1,400 monthly mortgage payment on her three-family house in Dorchester. Yet NACA had no qualms about arranging the $137,500 mortgage in the first place, notwithstanding the fact that Swain-Price's husband was in prison, that she'd had previous credit problems, and that the monthly mortgage payment constituted more than half her monthly salary. The fact that NACA has arranged an agreement to forestall foreclosure does not inspire confidence that she will have the resources required to maintain her aging frame house: her new monthly payment, in recognition of previously missed payments, is $1,879.

Even if all the CRA-related loans marketed by nonprofits were to turn out fine, the CRA system is still troubling. Like affirmative action, it robs the creditworthy of the certain knowledge that they have qualified by dint of their own effort for a first home mortgage, a milestone in any family's life. At the same time it sends the message that this most important milestone has been provided through the beneficence of government, devaluing individual accomplishment. Perhaps the Clinton White House viewed this as a costless way to use the banking system to create a new crop of passionate Democratic loyalists, convinced that CRA has delivered them from an uncaring Mammon—when, in all likelihood, banks would have been eager to have most of them as customers, regulation or no.

CRA also serves to enforce misguided views about how cities should develop, or redevelop. Consider the "investment" criterion—the loans to commercial borrowers rather than individual home buyers—that constitutes 25 percent of the record on which banks are judged in their compliance review. The Comptroller of the Currency's office makes clear that it is not interested in just any sort of investment in so-called underserved neighborhoods. Investment in a new apartment building or shopping center might not count if it would help change a poor neighborhood into a more prosperous one, or if it is not directly aimed at serving those of low income. Regulators want banks to invest in housing developments built through non-profit community development corporations. Banks not only receive CRA credit for such "investment"—which they can make anywhere in the country, not just in their back-yard—they also receive corporate tax credits for it through the Low Income Housing Tax Credit. Banks have little in-centive to make sure such projects are well managed, since they get their tax credits and CRA credits up front.

This investment policy misunderstands what is good for cities and for the poor. Cities that are alive are cities in flux, with neighborhoods rising and falling as tastes and eco-nomies change. This ceaseless flux is a process, as Jane Jacobs brilliantly described it in *The Economy of Cities*, that fuels investment, creates jobs, and sparks innovative adaptation of older buildings to new purposes. Those of modest means benefit both from the new jobs and from being able to rent or purchase homes in once expensive neighborhoods that take on new roles. The idea that it is necessary to flash-freeze certain neighborhoods and set them aside for the poor threatens to disrupt urban vitality and the renewal that comes from the individual plans and efforts of a city's people.

But keeping these neighborhoods forever poor is the CRA vision. The CRA will help virtually any lower-income family who can come close to affording a mortgage pay-ment to purchase a home, often in a nonpoor neighbor-hood. Thanks to CRA-driven bank investment, poor neighborhoods would then fill up with subsidized rental complexes, presumably for those poor families who can't earn enough even to get a subsidized, easy credit mortgage. The effects of all this could be to undermine lower-middle-class neighborhoods by introducing families not prepared for home ownership into them, leaving behind poor neighborhoods in which low-income apartments, filled with the worst-off and least competent, stand alone—hardly a recipe for renewal.

The CRA firmly linked itself to the Clinton administration and powerfully serves Democratic party interests. When Senator Gramm attacked the CRA for its role in funding advocacy groups and for the burden it imposes on banks, the Clinton administration fought back furiously, willing to let the crucial Financial Services Modernization Act, to which Gramm had attached his CRA changes, die unless Gramm dropped demands that, for instance, CRA reviews become less frequent. In the end, Gramm, despite his key position as the chairman of the Senate Committee on Banking, Housing, and Urban Affairs (even the committee's name reflects a CRA consciousness) and his willingness to hold repeal of the Glass-Steagal Act hostage to CRA reform, could manage only to require community groups to make public their agreements with banks, disclosing the size of their loan commitments and fees.

Our new president should push for outright abolition of the CRA. Failing that, he could simply instruct the Treasury to roll back the compliance criteria to their more relaxed, pre-Clintonian level. But to make the case for repeal—and ensure that some future Democratic president couldn't simply reimpose Clinton's rules—he might test the basic premise of the Community Reinvestment Act: that the banking industry serves the rich, not the poor. He could carry out a controlled experiment requiring no CRA lending in six Federal Reserve districts, while the CRA remains in force in six others. A comparison of lending records would show whether there is any real case for the CRA. In addition, CRA regulators should require nonprofit groups with large CRA-related loan commitments to track and report foreclosure and delinquency rates. For it is these that will reflect the true threat that the CRA poses, a threat to the health of cities.

[2000]

# FIVE

..................................................

# Don't Let CDCs Fool You

Conventional wisdom about cities has it that community development corporations (CDCs) are one of the great successes of urban policy, responsible for sparking a revival of inner-city neighborhoods across the nation. The CDC movement, now three decades old, gets credit for physically upgrading shabby neighborhoods and also for uplifting the poor who live in them by organizing them to help themselves. CDCs, write Paul Grogan and Tony Proscio in *Comeback Cities*—a new bible of the CDC movement and a book that ranks CDCs ahead even of improved public safety in helping to bring back cities—are "citizen-formed self-help groups trying to revitalize their own neighborhoods." These bootstrap operations, write Grogan and Proscio, are the answer to the question: "If government on its own has repeatedly failed to save inner cities, who can save them?" Such rhetoric has helped make CDCs popular left, right, and center.

Without doubt CDCs can point to apartment buildings they've had a hand in building or renovating and supermarkets they've helped recruit to inner-city locations. And, true, local residents serve on their boards of directors. But, fundamentally, the methods of the movement are not what its organizers claim them to be, and the movement's impact is not a healthy one. Rather than being true grassroots groups, CDCs add up to a cleverly decentralized HUD, almost entirely financed through federal funding and provisions of the federal tax code, not through the assets and initiative of neighborhood residents. CDCs are in fact a sub-rosa version of the 1960s War on Poverty, built on that era's false assumptions that, since "the system" necessarily conspires to keep the poor in poverty, only political action can ameliorate their condition. Or, as the National Congress for Community Economic Development (NCCED), the trade group for the CDC "industry," revealingly puts it: "CDCs are helping to empower millions of people *left out of* the economic mainstream" (emphasis added).

These organizations threaten to maintain the poor in a dependency that runs counter to the new spirit of welfare reform. Rather than encouraging upward mobility and genuine self-reliance, the implicit message of the CDC movement to the poor is: stay put and organize for government benefits. As a result, CDCs are bad for cities; like the public housing they claim to supersede and improve upon, they threaten to keep the poor frozen in poverty and cities forever frozen as warehouses for the eternally poor. Rather than representing a true urban revival, CDC neighborhoods are Potemkin villages, sustained by government resources and outside organizers, and potentially impeding the new, spontaneous development that is the hallmark of urban vitality.

Today's CDC "industry," as insiders insist on calling it, is huge, consisting of some 3,600 such organizations heavily concentrated in the Northeast and Midwest and on the West Coast. More than fifty are in New York, more than twenty in Boston. They proliferated during the Clinton years, increasing by 64 percent between 1995 and 1999 alone. They are not corporations in the normal sense, of course, but nonprofit organizations, run by paid employees, not by a volunteer corps of engaged citizens, though they claim to speak for the neighborhood around them and are generally housed in small storefronts or converted apartments in the midst of their modest neighborhood domains. Over the past twenty years, they have, through direct and indirect federal subsidies, built more than 500,000 units of low-rent (though often high-cost) housing—nearly half as many apartments as the entire existing stock of U.S. public housing.

Although they struggle to sound politically centrist, CDCs cling unambiguously to the left end of the spectrum. The theme of the recent annual NCCED convention, for example, was "Community Economic Development Equals Economic Justice," and one speaker, evidently reflecting the views of his large, enthusiastic audience, referred to newly "selected" President Bush. Walk into local CDC offices and you feel like you've entered a 1960s time warp. A bulletin board at the Urban Edge CDC office in Boston's Roxbury section, for instance, advertises a job opening at the local chapter of "Bikes Not Bombs." A placard at the Fifth Avenue Committee, a CDC in Brooklyn's Park Slope, proclaims, "Our mission is to advance social and economic justice in South Brooklyn." The Fifth Avenue Committee sponsored a campaign opposing Giuliani administration policies that required some welfare recipients to work in public jobs, and it supports a "campaign of conscience" to generate "community solidarity" in favor of a "displacement-free zone" in South Brooklyn.

Such campaigns, and the core activities of CDCs generally, reflect beliefs about cities and the poor that have not really changed since the 1960s—even as prosperity has vastly lowered unemployment and brought millions of the poor into the workforce. CDCs operate on the implicit Marxist belief that "the system" will exclude a significant number of people from adequate reward for their labor, or from the chance for meaningful employment in the first place; these people—in effect, the army of surplus labor that Marx believed would always exist in order to keep a steady downward pressure on wages—need permanent protection. Their neighborhoods should, as a matter of "economic justice," be made more pleasant through subsidized renovated housing, and for the same reason they must be protected against displacement by gentrification. To suggest that this army of surplus labor might adapt and prosper on its own is a cruel mockery.

CDC theorists inherited these deeply pessimistic views from the 1960s social planners who created HUD, on the belief that private market forces would never be drawn to restore poor urban neighborhoods or to create jobs in them, and that therefore government must provide both income support and housing for the poor trapped in cities. As early as 1969 the economists John Kain and Joseph Persky recognized the perniciousness of this view: they cautioned that the earliest CDCs (and federal efforts to rebuild the inner city generally) didn't encourage upward mobility but instead were merely attempts to "gild the ghetto"—while keeping it a ghetto. In this spirit, fundamental to the CDC project, *Comeback Cities* author Grogan has asserted that, in improving the lives of the poor, it makes sense for housing to "come first."

Far from representing the break with big-government anti-poverty programs that its advocates represent it to be, the CDC movement came into existence—quite self-consciously—to be a better-managed, clandestine continuation of the War on Poverty, designed by one of the original architects of the Johnson administration's war. The late Mitchell Sviridoff, a onetime Detroit union organizer and welfare chief in John Lindsay's administration in New York, had, as an aide to the mayor of New Haven in the early 1960s, made that city the leading advertisement for the Ford Foundation's Gray Areas Program—the first effort to invest massive outside funds in the rebuilding of ghettos by giving grants to community groups. The Gray Areas Program became the template for the Johnson administration's Model Cities Program. As a student in Sviridoff's "Workshop on Urban Blight" in 1982 at Princeton's Woodrow Wilson School, I watched him flesh out the CDC blueprint he had created shortly before, while he was at the end of his long stint as a Ford Foundation program officer.

A hard-boiled but realistic man of the left, Sviridoff had accepted two key critiques of the War on Poverty—those of Daniel Patrick Moynihan, who dismissed Model Cities as fractious, politically confrontational, and corrupt in his book *Maximum Feasible Misunderstanding*, and of Edward Banfield, who identified the underclass as the real threat to life in poor neighborhoods in his classic *The Unheavenly City*. In Sviridoff's new CDC model, rigorous screening of tenants would avoid the problems Banfield had identified. Strict financial accountability—by an outside overseer—would prevent the waste and corruption of Model Cities. To perform this function, just before he left the Ford Foundation, Sviridoff had funded something called the Local Initiatives Support Corporation (LISC), designed to funnel foundation money directly to newly forming CDCs—often in the form of loans, so as to encourage businesslike operations among the recipients. Sviridoff himself became LISC's president. While the methods were a new wrinkle, the overall goal of Sviridoff's movement was the same as the War on Poverty's: stable poor neighborhoods—that is, poor neighborhoods made stable for their present populations through physical improvement financed by outside funds.

The financing system for the CDC movement's hundreds of thousands of units of subsidized housing is a marvel of what federal officials like to call "off-budget" financing. The linchpin of the system is the Low Income Housing Tax Credit, legislated by Congress in 1986 and made permanent in 1993. This device offers a dollar-for-dollar tax reduction to those who "invest" in subsidized low-income housing. Corporations looking to limit their tax liability while publicizing apparent good works flock to the Low Income Housing Tax Credit. How do a myriad of small, local CDCs get matched up with big corporations looking to make such investments? Here's where the Local Initiatives Support Corporation comes in. LISC—where Paul Grogan succeeded Mitchell Sviridoff as president in 1987—makes the match between those looking for tax relief and individual CDCs.

Banks are especially eager to play this game, not because CDCs are good investments but because of pressure
from federal regulators through the Community Reinvestment Act (see Chapter Four). The act (which the Clinton
administration vigorously enforced) calls on banks to direct funds to so-called underserved areas—in other words,
areas where it doesn't pay, in real financial terms, for them
to invest. The threat of regulatory sanction—particularly,
delays in merger approvals—leads banks eagerly to seek
good Community Reinvestment Act "ratings" and thus to
enter into much-ballyhooed "public-private partnerships"
with CDCs, which are said (in a complimentary David
Broder column in the *Washington Post*, for instance) to
"leverage" private funds. It may be no coincidence that, in
addition to his executive duties at the banking and financial services giant Citigroup, former Clinton administration
treasury secretary Robert Rubin has, as his community
service, become the chairman of LISC. Nor is it any coincidence that, according to the NCCED, 28 percent of CDCs
engage in pro–Community Reinvestment Act "advocacy."

So it is that CDCs raise capital. But they can't typically
raise enough this way—Low Income Housing Tax Credits
assigned to the states by the IRS based on state population
are limited. CDCs typically raise additional development
capital through low-interest mortgages made available to
them by state housing finance agencies. These public authorities borrow at below-market interest rates and funnel
the proceeds to CDCs.

Even such low-interest mortgages must be paid back,
however. That means collecting the rent every month. Here,
old-fashioned federal spending comes into play: HUD's Section 8 housing voucher program typically pays the monthly

rent on CDC apartments. HUD normally sets rent levels incredibly high—which allows CDCs to pay their staffs and
meet expenses. One Boston CDC director recently crowed
to me about his success in persuading HUD to set the "fair
market" rent for the CDC-owned apartments in his low-income neighborhood at no less than $2,300 a month.

The government-created combination of tax credits,
bank regulation, and rent subsidies has proved to be a financing juggernaut, a stealth housing production program
ideal for the era in which big government was supposedly
over. Between 1995 and 1998, CDCs used the system to
build 300,000 units of new subsidized housing. Although
the NCCED likes to trumpet the number of jobs and apartments CDCs have "created" this way, they do so only by
using the power of government to divert funds from other,
probably more productive, investments. Beneath the illu-
sion of market-based investment is the reality of the coer-
cion of private capital.

The CDC financing juggernaut can be as lucrative as it
is effective. Subsidized, no-risk development generates
large developers' fees for CDCs during the construction
process and high management fees thereafter. Take, for example, the proposed renovation of a twenty-eight-unit
apartment building recently approved for tax credits by the
Massachusetts Housing Finance Agency. Actual construction costs will be $133,000 per unit. But the total costs will
be much higher: $248,000 per unit, with much of the ex-
cess—$33,000 per unit for acting as general contractor,
$27,000 per unit in "fees and overhead"—going into the
CDC's coffers.

What's wrong with this? Just because CDCs misrepre-
sent themselves as far more bootstrap-based than they re-

ally are, is their activity—the Sorcerer's Apprentice–like production of nonprofit-run subsidized housing—problematic? The answer is yes.

As with public housing and other philanthropic housing projects in the past, there's always the danger of insufficient maintenance. Warning signs of bad maintenance, along with full-blown maintenance problems, have already turned up in CDC buildings. Most CDCs apparently are not putting enough aside for looming repairs. On-Site Insight, a private firm specializing in such assessments, recently examined 102 properties in the "affordable housing" stock and found that "seven out of ten developments face unmet capital needs." It judged that CDCs should set aside at least $2,200 more per unit per year for maintenance and repairs and that CDCs owning older buildings, where maintenance needs loom larger, should set aside even more. CDC advocates acknowledge this problem. Francie Ferguson of the Neighborhood Reinvestment Corporation, a federal entity established to assist nonprofit housing developers, observes: "The assumption is that the hard thing to do is to get housing built. In fact, the hard thing is to run it well."

The details of deferred maintenance can be chilling. An extreme case is the South Bronx group called Banana Kelly Community Improvement Association, one of the original CDCs Sviridoff funded through LISC. This year LISC had to foreclose on fourteen Banana Kelly buildings and seek other management because, as the *New York Times* put it, "Its buildings have deteriorated; tenants have complained of no heat, of rats, of repairs not done. . . . 866 Beck Street is a building so badly deteriorated that it had to be vacated." The *Times*'s excellent June 2000 series about the organization—which *Comeback Cities* featured as a "block club turned builder"—quoted a Bronx community board member and Banana Kelly tenant who said, "Our savior has become a slumlord."

Or consider the example of a Boston development called Tent City, born out of a protest group's occupation of vacant land by tents to dramatize what it saw as the need for subsidized housing. The Massachusetts Housing Finance Agency's 1999 assessment of Tent City's condition found the following, according to an internal agency memo: "Eight roofs had active leaks. Carbon monoxide was at unacceptable levels because of poor maintenance of the ventilation system." Despite all the CDC rhetoric about grassroots oversight, the project had hired a private security firm, but it was "not performing up to standards" and lacked a working relationship with the Boston police, *the latter critical given the past history of youth gangs and drugs*" (emphasis added). Again, despite all the rhetoric of community control, Tent City had also contracted out its overall maintenance—like 41 percent of all CDCs.

Yet the maintenance issue isn't what's most worrisome about CDCs (and so far, many appear well maintained). The real worry focuses on the people who actually live in CDC housing. Just like old-fashioned public housing projects, the new subsidized accommodations mostly house single mothers, who are the main recipients of the Section 8 rent subsidies on which CDC financing relies. (Only 8 percent of households receiving rent vouchers are families with children with both spouses present.) In other words, rather than being an authentic breakthrough in building healthy communities for working families, CDCs are just part of the vast financial support system for illegitimacy, with all its bad effects for both mothers and their children.

Because CDC staffers misunderstand the reason their tenants are poor—blaming supposed injustices in the economic system rather than the bad life decisions of welfare mothers—they're involved in preserving the old welfare culture that the 1996 welfare reforms have begun to supersede. CDCs, doggedly faithful to their rhetoric about "stable" neighborhoods, don't urge their tenants to move up and out. Urban Edge estimates that at least half its tenants have already stayed ten years or longer. Brooklyn's Fifth Avenue Committee reports "almost no turnover." As with all public and subsidized housing, CDCs place no time limit on how long one can retain one's subsidy after initially qualifying. Indeed, subsidized rent can seduce even ambitious tenants to limit their impulse toward self-improvement. At one Urban Edge property I met two women, board members of the organization, who both said that, had their building not been renovated—allowing them to live in an upgraded apartment at low rent—they would have gone out and bought their own homes.

Even apart from their stable-neighborhood ideology, CDCs have a financial incentive not to urge their tenants to move up and out. They need the poor, and the generous subsidized rents they bring with them, to pay their own bills. When Urban Edge recently completed a new building, for instance, it couldn't find enough qualified or interested potential tenants in its immediate neighborhood. So the organization—officially dedicated to neighborhood comeback—imported poor tenants, primarily single mothers, from other, poorer parts of the city. Here is a dismal underside to the CDC story: the finances of their projects depend on there always being a stream of poor, subsidized households.

Incredibly, CDC financing arrangements explicitly assume a steady supply of such households. Massachusetts, for instance, continues to build subsidized housing in Boston based on the following logic: because 32 percent of the city's households are low income, the state should continue to support subsidized housing construction until 32 percent of all Boston units are "affordable." (The current figure is over 20 percent.) Thus the state officially does not foresee the possibility of upward mobility. It assumes a static economy in which cities are not starting points for ambitious strivers of modest means but long-term poorhouses.

This construction of stealth public housing is not only bad for the poor but is also a sure way to inhibit a real comeback in older city neighborhoods. Cities bounce back when decline makes their land so cheap that it becomes economic for businesses to buy. CDCs claim, on the contrary, that it is their housing activities that set the stage for growth, attracting subsequent private investment. But Harvard University social scientist Sara Stoutland has found that "there is no hard evidence of such a widespread 'spillover effect.'" In fact the "spillover effects" of CDCs are much more likely to be negative than positive, hindering urban economic revival. To take one example out of thousands upon thousands, a fledgling Internet-related firm called Virtual Access Networks recently decided to build its new corporate headquarters in the depressed mill town of Lawrence, Massachusetts—a place in the mold of Bridgeport, Camden, or Buffalo. Why Lawrence? The firm says it looked for the least expensive space that was most convenient for the largest number of its employees. Lawrence should count itself fortunate that some CDC had not beaten

Virtual Access Networks to the site and turned it into more housing for the poor—housing that the struggling city already has in superabundance.

The nonhousing activities of CDCs also have a way of backfiring economically. Some seven hundred CDCs nationwide own and operate nonprofit businesses, on the assumption that, since the larger economic system keeps the poor permanently poor, they must be cared for in a separate, "compassionate," noncapitalist economy. In this spirit, Brooklyn's Fifth Avenue Committee operates Ecomat Cleaners, "an environmentally friendly solution to toxic dry cleaning," with ten employees—and an annual loss, subsidized by foundations and by housing-related income. Occasionally such subsidized ventures have proven disastrous. In Indianapolis, Eastside Investments, a CDC once held up as a national exemplar, effectively went bankrupt—shrinking from eighty employees to four—largely as the result of costs associated with a business it started. Here was the separate economy with a vengeance: Eastside was going to manufacture building materials for use in its own subsidized housing projects. The factory would provide employment for the people living in its units. Instead the CDC lost $800,000 on "Shelter Systems." But the fundamental problem with all such enterprises lies in their conception, not their performance. During a period in which unemployment hit historical lows, CDCs continued to operate on the assumption that it was necessary to develop an alternative, nonprofit economy to shelter the poor, much like sheltered workshops for the blind or retarded.

CDCs often manage their other nonhousing economic development activities poorly too, including their business of renting commercial space to for-profit firms. The director of a Central Harlem credit union, for instance, complains that a nearby CDC has left a block of storefronts empty and boarded up. He suspects that their housing development provides such a reliable level of income with relatively little effort that, he says, they "don't want the hassle" of finding commercial tenants.

But without a doubt CDCs have also been able to recruit some successful for-profit businesses to their neighborhoods. It's great to see a new Key Food across from the Fifth Avenue Committee office and a new McDonald's in the mini-mall built and leased by Urban Edge in Boston. But one must ask the question: why are such intermediaries necessary for inner-city development when they are unneeded in the broader commercial economy? If land is available, zoning flexible, and permits easy to get, if there is unmet demand for a new supermarket or restaurant, and if police are doing their job of allowing business owners to operate safely, business will take root as it does anywhere else. Indeed, right nearby the McDonald's that Urban Edge recruited to Roxbury, two major national drugstore chains, Walgreen's and CVS, opened new stores without any help from a CDC.

Only in the context of the protest politics so often found in inner-city neighborhoods—the knee-jerk response against chain stores or outsiders—do CDCs make sense. They provide the means for investors to buy entrée and community support. Urban Edge, for instance, agreed to rent a storefront to McDonald's only if the fast-food giant signed a lease agreeing to share profits with the CDC—even though the store was on land leased by the state to Urban Edge at minimal cost. Says Urban Edge executive director Mossik Hacobian: "Why should we let profits generated by our community make someone in Chicago rich? We think at least some of that money should go to the community itself." The arbiter of how that money should be used is, of course, Urban Edge—although, concedes Hacobian, there is nothing in the agreement with McDonald's that specifies exactly how the money will improve the community. (Urban Edge says it has used the funds to build premises it rents to a Boys and Girls Club.) Moreover, this vision overlooks a great many things—not only the fact that McDonald's is a public corporation in which Roxbury residents (through pension funds, for instance) might actually have a stake, but the fact that McDonald's already supports the community the old-fashioned way, by providing a needed service and needed jobs, and paying property taxes.

Of course, elected officials accountable to the voters oversee the spending of those taxes, but to whom are CDCs accountable? Although these organizations are nominally under the control of boards of directors that include community residents, neighborhoods as a whole have no formal means to oversee or direct them. In fact occasionally a CDC will explicitly ignore what it takes to be the majority view in a neighborhood. The Fifth Avenue Committee—which has grown from eight employees in 1992 to forty today—decided last year against neighborhood-based elections for its board of directors. Board members feared, in part, that newcomers from middle-class Park Slope might take over the organization and move it off its mission, which includes "combating displacement caused by gentrification." The fear was that residents might instead work for standard neighborhood improvements, such as better parks and schools. Instead of permitting an open election, Fifth Avenue Committee bylaws actually dictate specific racial and income quotas on its board. "At all times, a majority of the board members will be people of color. At all times, a majority of board members will be people who currently are or at some time in the past have been low-income. At least 30 percent of the board will be people who are currently low-income."

How can an outfit with "community" in its name get away with excluding certain classes of local residents? The Fifth Avenue Committee's director of community organizing candidly puts it this way: "There is a very small subset of funders that is concerned about accountability issues. Most other funders just sort of like us because we're a CDC. By definition, we do good things, and that's good enough for them."

Foundation funders believe that they are supporting projects conceived and refined by low-income community residents. In reality, CDC directors are middle-class professionals. The Fifth Avenue Committee and Urban Edge both have office staffs dominated by local residents—mostly black and Hispanic—but both are run by white professionals with degrees from elite universities. Judging by the attendance at the NCCED Washington convention, many black professionals hold CDC executive jobs too; this seems to be another quasi-public-sector career path that attracts capable African Americans, already so overrepresented in the public sector.

But the lack of neighborhood oversight and strong outside board members can also lead to the old War on Poverty problem: corruption. Banana Kelly—founded in 1978 with the quintessential CDC motto: "Don't Move, Improve"—is the poster child here, its financial records subpoenaed by the New York State attorney general and one of its employees reportedly interviewed by the FBI and the New York City Department of Investigation. Writes the *New York Times*: Banana Kelly's "finances have become chaotic. Some board members and former employees have raised questions about how government money was used and about the form in which [chairwoman Yolanda Rivera] is compensated." With the organization so cash-strapped that its offices lacked toilet paper, the *Times* reported, chairwoman Rivera used "part of the organization's dwindling resources—what she calls general, or unrestricted funds—to pay for travel, including a trip to a conference in Kenya for her and several associates."

CDC advocates continually imply that theirs is a true volunteer movement—"a uniquely American force in the best traditions of the social and economic institutions observed by Alexis de Tocqueville in early-nineteenth-century communities," as the NCCED puts it. Yet among themselves, CDC advocates acknowledge that subsidized building renovation does not inherently create Tocquevillian ties that bind. Hence they have hatched the so-called community building movement, which seeks self-consciously to organize the neighborhood structures—block clubs, crime watches, recreation leagues—that arise spontaneously where residents pay their own rent or mortgage and feel responsible for their environs. The community building of the CDC world attempts to professionalize all that—to use hired organizers and paid advocates as substitutes for Tocquevillian community institutions.

Congressional Republicans have fallen for CDCs hook, line, and sinker. In the waning days of the Clinton administration, the Republican Congress hugely pumped up the key engine of the CDC explosion, the Low Income Housing

Tax Credit, from $1.25 per capita per state to $1.50 for 2001, $1.75 for 2002—and indexed to inflation for subsequent years. CDCs are salivating at such new federal pots as the "New Markets Initiative"—a subsidized tax-credit-supported approach to commercial development. As the LISC website puts it, ominously: "The New Markets Tax Credit promises to be as valuable for community-sponsored economic development as the Low Income Housing Tax Credit has been for rental housing development." If it brings the same sort of investment based not on assessment of markets but, instead, on brownie points for various kinds of "social responsibility," this is bad news for cities, where good policing has already sparked commercial development in poor neighborhoods. Further bad news is *Comeback Cities* author Grogan's recent formation of a group called CEOs for Cities, which seeks increased support of businessmen for CDC subsidy schemes.

Instead of falling for such stuff, Congress and the Bush administration should begin doing everything they can do to bring inner-city neighborhoods into the mainstream economy. They should put time limits on the Section 8 rental vouchers that are the CDCs' lifeblood, and so try to weaken the movement. And they should encourage and help cities to spark revival the old-fashioned ways: by providing safe streets, effective schools, attractive parks, and work-oriented, values-laden social programs. Cities must help themselves too, by controlling costs, lowering taxes, minimizing regulation, and encouraging private housing and commercial development. Shortcuts like CDCs are doomed to be dead ends.

[2001]

# SIX

·············································

# How Charlotte Is Revolutionizing Public Housing

Several years on, the 1996 Welfare Reform Act has brought encouraging results that even most of its early supporters could scarcely have hoped for: welfare rolls cut in half and former welfare mothers moving into the workforce with the seeds of a new work ethic and fresh optimism about the future. Yet one thing threatens, if not to derail welfare reform, at least to slow its progress and blunt its full beneficial impact: the nation's vast public housing system, sheltering exactly the same people whom welfare reform targets—unwed mothers, whose fatherless families have proved incubators of social pathology. Although welfare reform is pushing many public housing residents into the workforce, public housing's perverse incentive structure will probably impel many of them to settle permanently for a first low-wage job instead of embracing upward mobility wholeheartedly. And though scattering these families, as some housing reformers have urged, surely can't by itself change their values, it's also true that concentrating them in permanently subsidized communities, where illegitimacy remains the unquestioned norm and work isn't seen as leading anywhere, can only make it harder for them to succeed.

That's why what's happening in Charlotte, North Carolina, is so important. With little fanfare, Charlotte's public housing authority is providing a blueprint for transforming the nature of public housing or even, over the long term, phasing it out. The key to Charlotte's new approach is time limits. This simple idea promises to make public housing more like the new welfare system—short-term aid, provided on the assumption of the recipient's serious effort to improve her situation. "What we're saying over and over again to our residents," explains Charlotte Housing Authority chief executive officer Harrison Shannon, Jr., "is 'in, up, and out.'" Charlotte, in other words—along with a tiny handful of the nation's 3,200 public housing authorities—is thus seeking to make public housing policy reinforce welfare reform's message of self-reliance rather than weaken it.

A time limit for public housing, extending welfare reform's ethic of personal responsibility, represents an historic break with the fundamental misconception that inspired the construction of public housing from the start. Public housing grew out of the idea that the private housing market could never provide decent and sanitary housing for those of modest means. In this conception—articulated by Catherine Bauer in her influential 1936 *Modern Housing* and embraced by President Franklin D. Roosevelt in the National Housing Act of 1937—public housing authorities were to run apartment buildings as permanent public utilities, with publicly financed construction keeping rents low.

It's hard to exaggerate how mistaken this idea was, even when Bauer and other advocates first formulated it. From the end of the Civil War until 1937, private builders had erected a dizzying variety of housing for the striving poor as they improved their condition over time (see Chapter One). Chicago witnessed the construction of 211,000 decent, inexpensive two-family homes during those years—21 percent of the city's total residences. Private builders fabricated no fewer than 300,000 affordable, livable row houses in Philadelphia during the five decades prior to 1930. To be sure, a temporary shortage of privately built housing after World War II meant that many blue-collar families briefly benefited from public housing. But dynamic postwar economic growth left Bauer's argument in tatters: two-income working families flocked to the economical, privately built subdivisions of the suburbs. Today an astounding two-thirds of American households aren't renters at all—they own their own homes. It's hard to find evidence that the nation ever needed its public housing system.

As those working-class families headed for the suburbs in the fifties, public housing began its transformation into latter-day poorhouses. Federal legislation authored by the late Massachusetts Republican senator Edward Brooke accelerated and intensified the change. The 1968 Brooke Amendment, seeking to protect low-income earners from local housing authority rent hikes, mandated that public housing households pay no more than one-third of their income in rent—but it also required them to pay no less than that third. This law should claim a prize for unintended consequences. It drove from public housing the remaining working families, whose rents suddenly shot up now that they had to pay a third of their incomes to the housing authority. They could now do better in the private housing market. At the same time the Brooke Amendment opened the door wide to single mothers on public assistance; they'd pay very little.

If always unnecessary, public housing now became truly pernicious. It became a crucial part of the welfare-support network that abetted young women in having illegitimate children. It told young women that if they had a baby out of wedlock, they could leave home and set up their own apartments on the public dime. In a 1989 HUD survey, the most frequent reason single mothers gave for moving into public housing was "to establish own housing." Public housing's complicity in fostering single-parent families is so troubling because of what we now know about illegitimacy. Having a child out of wedlock often sentences the mother to poverty: 68 percent of single-parent families are poor, and single parents head 90 percent of black families in poverty. Worse, the children in those families suffer dismayingly high levels of social pathology, from school dropout to criminality.

Today 40 percent of all low-income single-parent families—26 percent of all poor families in the country—reside in 507,000 of the nation's 1.3 million public housing apartments and more than 1 million of the 2.7 million units of other publicly subsidized housing (mostly paid for with federal Section 8 housing vouchers). Single mothers and their kids occupy 39 percent of all public housing apartments, the biggest demographic group in the system. Only the elderly, occupying 32 percent, come close. And since the elderly usually live together in buildings set aside just for them, low-income single-parent families dominate many housing projects.

Public housing is where the long-term welfare recipients wound up and stayed. In Charlotte's large projects, 40 percent of households have stayed five years or more; 20 percent have stayed ten years or more. Some dependent families have lived in Charlotte's system for three generations. It's little different elsewhere. The average stay of tenants in public housing nationally is eighty months; in New York, ninety-nine months—just over eight years. And because 9 percent of tenants leave every year, those averages mask a sizable core of households that stay even longer.

Charlotte's time limits propose to change all this radically. The city's public housing authority currently enrolls more than five hundred of its eighteen hundred nonelderly households in its "Transitional Family" program, an innovative initiative launched in the late 1980s that combines voluntary time limits with counseling, education, and financial management to encourage public housing residents to become self-sufficient. To get residents to agree to the time limits and take other real steps toward self-improvement, Charlotte offers a powerful incentive: newer, more desirable housing. The authority can get away with its system of incentives and disincentives because, as HUD rules have traditionally demanded, it still guarantees low-income residents public housing—but in its typically rundown, disorderly high-rise projects, not in its nicest buildings. Any large-scale public housing authority in the country could easily follow Charlotte's lead in navigating creatively around HUD requirements.

A resident who wants to move up from the shabby, conventional projects into the much nicer, relatively new Victoria Square and Claremont complexes must accept a voluntary five-year limit on her tenure in public housing and must already have shown her seriousness about self-improvement by starting to work on her high school equivalency certificate or signing up for community college or job-training courses. To remain in the nicer housing or to hope to move on to something better, she must meet regularly with a social worker, who makes sure she's working toward obtaining both employment and an education. If she isn't, the program sends her back to the less desirable traditional housing.

An interesting innovation: but Charlotte's experiment gets even more creative than this. To push residents even closer toward self-sufficiency, Charlotte takes advantage of HUD's multi-billion-dollar public housing rebuilding project, Hope VI, in ways that the federal agency "absolutely never intended," as one candid HUD official admits, but that nevertheless are not forbidden.

The federal program, on its own terms, is decidedly unpromising. It frees up money to raze older, dilapidated public housing projects—usually forbidding high-rises—and to replace them with town houses mixed in among single-family homes and middle-income apartments. Hope VI makes the erroneous assumption, which has typified the thinking of public housing advocates since the days of Catherine Bauer, that one's housing environment determines one's behavior. If only poor, dysfunctional families could live next door to striving, middle-income families, this assumption runs, the good example would rub off and inspire the poor to self-improvement. But this formulation gets things backward: it is far more likely that disordered families will drive good families to despair through their anti-social behavior than that good families will improve the behavior of the disordered. Good neighborhoods take root and blossom through the efforts of striving, upwardly mobile families who've sought to distinguish themselves, economically and spiritually, from those who don't share their upstanding values. Hope VI simply ignores this crucial insight.

Yet Charlotte has turned this dubious federal program to its own responsibility-building ends by using brand-new Hope VI apartments to reward residents who've taken big strides toward self-sufficiency. When Charlotte, using Hope VI funds, demolished its notorious Earle Village project just east of the city's downtown, it told longtime residents of the project that they would have no special entitlement to enter First Ward Place, the pleasant town house complex that was to replace Earle. Instead, to enter these new town houses, not only would a resident have to have agreed to the five-year time limit, but she'd also have to have finished high school, shown that she'd held a job continuously for at least the past year, and agreed to work with a social worker to budget her funds with an eye to moving up and out. Again, failure to continue moving forward means a quick return to traditional public housing.

Charlotte rewards the most successful strivers with the best housing of all. The housing authority runs four air-conditioned apartment complexes in some of the city's choicest, most crime-free residential neighborhoods, in the vicinity of good schools—complexes built just with city funds and thus free from HUD regulations, including the Brooke Amendment's one-third-of-income rent rule. To qualify for these buildings, a participant must not only accept the five-year limit, have her high school diploma, and be working, but she must also agree to pay a flat-rate rent that will not go down even if she loses her job. In other words, she must give up the Brooke Amendment's safety net. If her income rises, the authority increases her rent but puts the extra money she's now paying into an escrowed savings account. When the participant "graduates," she can use the money to help pay rent in the private market or put a down payment on a house. Those who fail to graduate by the time their five years are up, though, go back to dreary traditional public housing.

Charlotte's innovative program has produced some striking successes that show how time-limiting public housing can strengthen welfare reform's message of self-sufficiency. Consider Greta Greer, who entered Charlotte's public housing system as a young welfare mother in 1993. In 1996 welfare reform pushed her into the workforce, where she landed a low-paying job as a day-care assistant. But public housing kept her horizons low. Why try to move up? After all, she had her apartment, and if she made more money, her rent would increase. She'd only get to keep sixty-six cents of every additional dollar. So why bother?

Greer's example confirms an old social science axiom about semi-dependency, familiar from the Seattle and Denver income-maintenance experiments of the 1970s: permanent subsidies are demoralizing and limit the long-term earnings of low-income workers. The Seattle and Denver studies on the effect of a negative income tax found that every dollar of subsidy given to low-income workers reduced their earnings from work by eighty cents, compared with workers without the subsidy.

Charlotte's time-limit program replaced Greer's diminished expectations with an invigorating sense of possibility. Agreeing to time limits in 1998, she moved into a better apartment. With the program's help, she learned how to check her credit rating and started to clear up bad debts. The program also encouraged her to get computer training and helped her prepare a résumé. She managed to get a better job as a receptionist in a collection agency, making ten dollars per hour. Newly confident, Greer began to interview in 1999 with several banks; First Union, one of Charlotte's largest employers, hired her. Greer now makes thirteen dollars per hour as an IRA specialist in the bank's investment department, has started a 401K plan, and is set to move her family out of public housing for their own home in a few months, well before her five-year limit is up.

Greer's seemingly successful exit from Charlotte's public housing is far from unique. More than 400 residents have used the Transitional Families program to move out between 1995 and 2000; 125 have bought their first houses thanks to the program over the same period. Would these residents eventually have left Charlotte public housing under the impetus of welfare reform alone, without the additional push from the time-limit program? Perhaps. But it is more likely, as Greer's early semi-dependency shows, that even in a welfare-reform environment, an unreformed public housing system will keep people from being all they can be.

Charlotte officials candidly acknowledge the need to separate families by attitude and achievement. "We don't want people who are trying to improve themselves to have neighbors from hell," says housing authority head Harrison Shannon. Charlotte's Transitional Families program supervisor, Janet Lynch, notes that rather than drawing inspiration from hardworking neighbors, the nonworking often try to undermine them. Cynthia Jackson, a public housing graduate, confirms it. "People were saying to me all the time, 'What are you doing? You'll never make it,'" she recalls. Lynch finds most inspirational those transitional families just starting the process of moving up—women who, still surrounded by the welfare culture, have made a commitment to change. "They form tight cliques for protection," Lynch observes. "They start off as fifteen strangers in a room and form a real bond; they swap baby-sitting, trade clothes, and form friendships I think will last." It's a heartening process to watch: the formerly dependent becoming a community of self-help and upward mobility.

Doubtless Charlotte could do more. The authority could, for example, forthrightly address the deepest problem of many program participants—having kids out of wedlock. Authority social worker Alicia Carr, for one, contends that many residents "aren't ready for marriage; they need to learn how to become independent and self-sufficient, first." But neither Carr nor the housing authority in general seems willing to ask whether these young women are ready for motherhood. Still, if one must choose between single mothers stuck in public housing and single mothers taking care of themselves and their families on their own, the choice is clear—all the more so if Charlotte's program helps discourage a new generation of single mothers by raising the aspirations of Greta Greer's children and the kids like them.

In Delaware the state public housing authority has just taken Charlotte's principle to its logical—if radical—conclusion: it has adopted a mandatory three-year time limit for all its nonelderly residents. Granted, Delaware's agency is tiny: it provides only twelve hundred units of public housing, sprinkled mostly across the rural chicken-processing belt of Sussex and Kent counties. But Delaware may foreshadow the future: Charlotte, a big urban housing authority, is considering adopting mandatory time limits too. As Harrison Shannon stresses, in refreshingly nonbureaucratic language, he doesn't want public housing to be a "safe harbor" for those who "lack a work ethic."

HUD regulations don't allow most housing authorities even to consider mandatory time limits. But Delaware and Charlotte are numbered among thirty-two housing authorities—1 percent of the national total—included in an HUD demonstration program called Moving to Work. HUD adopted the program under pressure from the 1996 Republican Congress, some of whose members were calling for the agency's outright abolition. Moving to Work regulations don't mention mandatory time limits specifically, but they don't prevent authorities from imposing them.

Delaware's program is tough stuff. Its mandatory time limit is shorter than Charlotte's voluntary one: just three years. Delaware helps residents find jobs and forces them to save money to start building a post–public housing nest egg, as Charlotte does. But any missteps—not showing up for work, failing to keep kids in school, even being late with the rent—lead to strikes against the resident. These expansively defined strikes represent failures to stay on the path of bourgeois social values that Delaware seeks to encourage. As in the national pastime, three strikes and you're out: the resident must either leave public housing or pay a higher, unsubsidized market rent to stay. There's no "traditional" public housing to fall back on.

Because Delaware's program departs so decisively from

past practices, it has angered some residents, who condemn it as unfair and punitive. But for others, the strict rules and firm guidance, as with welfare reform, help inculcate greater personal responsibility and a more vigorous work ethic. Linda Stephenson, who heads the tenant association in her housing authority complex, sees the new rules as eminently reasonable. "If I went to stay with my brother, he is going to want to know, 'What are you doing to better your situation? What are you going to do so you don't need my help?'" she notes. "That's how I see Moving to Work."

Critics of Delaware's initiative worry about what will happen to tenants after the three-year time limit expires. How will they afford market-level rents on the minimum wage? But the critics assume that the condition of the poor is static: that they will always be more or less dependent, incapable of taking charge of their own fates. After three years of training and support, critics assume, these public housing residents will still command only the minimum wage from employers. At least at present—with such a bustling national economy, and with welfare and housing reforms that aim to change the worldview of the poor and make them independent-minded—that assumption is suspect. Still, it is only prudent to acknowledge that, under such a no-nonsense regime, some residents ultimately will have to move back in with their parents or even seek a place in public shelters.

Over time, mandatory time limits could shrink the public housing system and ultimately end it as we know it. Delaware's time-limited tenants, for example, have the option, after their three years have expired, of remaining in their buildings and paying market-level rents. In the future, as apartments filled up with working families paying market rents, Delaware could sell off the now economically viable buildings to private buyers. Only a small core of emergency, time-limited housing would then remain. With housing time limits and welfare reform firmly in place, young women would be less tempted to become single mothers in the expectation of living on their own at public expense.

The value to cities of getting rid of public housing would be inestimable. Public housing projects haven't just incubated social pathology; they've also represented land held off the property-tax rolls and reserved in perpetuity for a specific low-value use. Freezing cities in this way is a sure way to sap their vitality: just look at how Harlem's thick concentration of public housing has kept the area from participating fully in the revitalization of Manhattan's Upper West Side. Putting public housing land back into circulation would help fuel economic growth.

Public housing has been a giant dead end. Charlotte and Delaware are showing the nation how it might extricate itself from a harmful system and set its demoralized inhabitants firmly on the road to the mainstream.

[2000]

...........................................

# Take
# Habitat for Humanity
# Seriously

It is easy to dismiss an organization that calls itself Habitat for Humanity. Worse, those who dislike Jimmy Carter can be put off by his high-profile volunteer carpentry in Habitat's cause of building houses for the poor, not to mention the fact that he once dedicated a Habitat house in Nicaragua with Daniel Ortega. Those skeptical of avowedly Christian organizations will be dismayed by Habitat founder and president Millard Fuller, the onetime Montgomery, Alabama, lawyer and direct-mail entrepreneur who starts each workday at the group's Americus, Georgia, headquarters with a mass devotion and is given to citing a biblical basis for the organization's no-interest loans to its home-buying families. (They are "partners in God" being helped by "Jesus economics.") Those who be-

lieve government alone can provide funds at the level necessary to create housing for the poor will view Habitat's use
of private donations and volunteer builders as naive. And
anyone skeptical about hype will be put off by the organization's propensity for media events: "blitz-builds" and
"Jimmy Carter workweeks," in which legions of volunteers
put up small houses for needy families in as little as six
hours. One blitz took place outside Miami's Joe Robbie Stadium as part of Super Bowl festivities.

But anyone concerned with contemporary American
housing and social policy ignores Habitat at his peril. At
the least, the sheer magnitude of this undertaking demands
it be taken seriously. "There is simply no way," observes
Millard Fuller, his six-foot-four frame squeezed behind the
desk in a makeshift modular office building at the sprawl-
ing Habitat headquarters complex, "that we will not be the
Number 1 home builder in the U.S. within four years."

Do not bet against this possibility. Habitat is a $160-
million-a-year enterprise, successfully raising funds both
through direct mail and corporate and foundation solicitation. A sophisticated media department in the group's renovated brick headquarters on the main drag in Americus
tracks press coverage. Habitat already has house-building
chapters in more than 1,100 American cities and towns, up
from 350 in 1991; it has built more than 125,000 houses to
date and is putting up 4,700 more a year, ranking it an estimated fourteenth among U.S. builders. Support comes not
only from individual volunteers pounding nails and laying
vinyl but from dozens of major national corporate sponsors
such as Dow Chemical, Black & Decker, and Popeye's
Chicken, which underwrite costs, donate tools and materials from storm doors and windows to foam insulation, and

encourage their employees to volunteer their time. Delta Air Lines encourages its customers to donate their frequent flyer miles to Habitat.

But it is not only for the sheer number of small, simple, low-cost new homes it is putting up that Habitat is note-worthy. Its methods are as notable as its product. It is, one might say, the Wal-Mart of American social policy. From its origins in the rural South it has spread nationwide, chal-lenging a range of previous ways of doing business—in this case the business of housing the poor and improving poor neighborhoods. It has offered a new vision of what type of housing assistance should be offered those of modest means, emphasizing ownership, not subsidized rentals. It has a new vision, too, of how those who become its "part-ners" ("not clients or recipients," insists Fuller) are chosen. Need is a prerequisite but is not sufficient; screening by cit-izen boards, generally with close links to local churches, is also required. Finally, Habitat has shown that a nonprofit organization, combining volunteers as well as a profes-sional staff, can succeed where government has largely failed in housing the poor—and in the process create a movement that is broadly and genuinely popular. More than twenty thousand Americans now serve on local Habi-tat boards of directors. Jimmy Carter and Bill Clinton are supporters—but so are Jack Kemp and Newt Gingrich, who wears an HFH lapel pin.

Notwithstanding the involvement of Carter and the presence of some other liberal atmospherics, it's hard to avoid seeing the exponential growth of Habitat as anything but a socially conservative movement that has taken deep hold—and that aspires, plausibly, to spread much more widely. Although rural in its origins, Habitat has established beachheads in Atlanta, Baltimore, Chicago, Cleveland, Newark, Oakland, and Philadelphia, and is poised to undertake an "urban initiative" to expand that reach even into New York. The city that invented U.S. public housing and has, more recently, spent as much as $100,000 per apartment to rehabilitate old buildings in bad neighborhoods—often giving priority to those with the most serious social problems—will find Habitat to be quite different in philosophy.

That philosophy is very much defined by Millard Fuller, the complex, late-middle-aged east Alabaman who founded Habitat in 1976. One might think of him as a New South version of Jacob Riis, the journalist whose exposés about Lower East Side tenements in the 1890s began America's march toward public housing. Fuller, like Riis, was distressed by the contrast between wealth and poverty epitomized by housing conditions. He deplored the southern version of the tenement: the shack, typically a one-room shanty, built of rough boards and roofed with corrugated metal, in which, Fuller recalls, black sharecroppers lived on his father's cotton farm in Lanett, Alabama, in the early 1940s. Fuller dreamed of ridding the world of such "poverty housing": the first of his four books about the Habitat philosophy is entitled *No More Shacks*.

As Fuller has described it, Habitat is the culmination of a very sixties-style cultural journey—from a comfortable life as a young entrepreneur to a search for meaning on a rural Georgia commune. It began when Fuller, a lanky, ambitious natural salesman, had established himself as a strikingly successful young lawyer and businessman in Montgomery, Alabama. While still a law student at the University of Alabama, Fuller and partner Morris Dees (an important figure in his own right who went on to found the influential, left-wing Southern Poverty Law Center) had established a series of businesses catering to student needs and supplying products for local organizations to sell in fund-raising drives. Fuller and Dees Enterprises continued to grow after the principals' graduation—to the point that Fuller had earned his first million by age twenty-five.

Despite his success—with all the trappings of a big brick house, a new Lincoln Continental, a cabin at the lake, and two thousand acres with cattle and horses—Fuller found that his marriage was floundering: his wife, Linda, then trying to finish college, was also raising their two preschool children largely on her own. "Millard came home for dinner," she recalls, "but that was about it. After he ate, it was right back to the office until 11 or midnight. I liked having the material things, but after a while they were a poor substitute for love and companionship." In 1965 his wife's abrupt retreat to New York and her threat to leave him for good prompted a crisis of faith in Fuller.

Beginning to question his single-minded pursuit of money, he found himself returning to the teachings about wealth, and about relations between rich and poor, that he had learned in his youth as an active churchgoer and church youth group member. He was drawn to the "social gospel"—the view, put forth by Walter Rauschenbusch in 1907 and commonplace in mainline Protestantism ever since, that the church has a role to play in addressing social conditions around it. In recent years groups like the National Council of Churches and the U.S. Catholic Conference have often acted as if the social gospel called mainly for advocacy on behalf of expansive government social welfare programs. By contrast, Rauschenbusch had emphasized personal, private efforts on behalf of the poor, such as the settlement-house movement pioneered by social gospel devotee Jane Addams, who went to "settle" among the poor so as to broaden her own horizons as well as those of new immigrants.

At last Fuller came to doubt whether wealth and a Christian life could coexist at all. "The emptier a person is on the inside," as he more recently wrote, "the more that person needs on the outside to compensate." After a tearful reunion with his wife, Fuller decided to sell off his interests in his businesses and "give the money away."

He spent the next two years as a fund-raiser for Alabama's historically black Tougaloo College. Then he happened—fatefully—to visit Koinonia Farm, a rural utopian experiment near the small Georgia city of Americus. Established in 1942, Koinonia was a most untraditional place for the South; its avowedly interracial character had led to violent encounters with neighbors. With a characteristically southern populist religious distrust for wealth, it sought to develop a cooperative, largely self-sufficient farm for both religious, altruistic whites and black former sharecroppers. Although the community had dwindled by the late sixties, it still cooperatively harvested fruits and pecans and sold them via mail order to a network of supporters. Perhaps it was the combination of religion and mail order that drew the Fullers. In 1968 they decided to move to Koinonia. It was there that Fuller's range of guises—from social gospel devotee to hardheaded mail-order empire builder—came together in the concept for Habitat for Humanity.

Koinonia's charismatic founder, pacifist Clarence Jordan, planted the seed of the idea. He had a dream of building several dozen simple homes, financed by interest-free mortgages, on the Koinonia grounds for neighbors then living in shacks. With Fuller's advice, Jordan established the Fund for Humanity and raised enough money through a direct-mail campaign to build eleven houses. After Jordan's death in 1969, the Fullers stayed on and supervised the building of the houses. In 1973 they went to Zaire for three years and built houses in rural villages. Upon their return Fuller decided to take the idea nationwide. "Is God glorified," Fuller wrote, "when a family builds for itself housing that is vastly in excess of what the legitimate needs are for that family? Or is God glorified more when a wealthy family exercises restraint, builds more modestly for its needs, and uses the excess funds to build additional modest houses for less fortunate families?"

In September 1976, Fuller founded Habitat for Humanity. The organization grew slowly, building 609 houses by the end of 1983. In 1984, showing the same drive and self-confidence that had made him such an accomplished entrepreneur, Fuller drove the eight miles from Habitat's headquarters in Americus to the nearby town of Plains, where he persuaded Jimmy Carter to lend his name and donate his time to a small, unknown regional organization—the turning point in Habitat's existence. Carter's participation in a most atypical Habitat event—the renovation of an apartment on Manhattan's Lower East Side—ignited the public interest in the previously obscure organization that sparked its phenomenal growth.

In devising the program, Fuller set out some inviolable ground rules: the houses must be well built but simple; they must be owned by the families who live in them; they must be built by both volunteers and the prospective owners themselves; the "partner" families must be screened by a

"family selection committee" and must pay back a mortgage over twenty years, though Habitat would not charge
interest. Finally, no government funds should go toward
the actual construction—although Habitat does accept government land and subsidies for infrastructure projects.

Fuller argues that the conventional welfare-state approach to housing robs the poor of their dignity. "The idea
had been for the government to do everything," he says.
"First we gave them high-rises; then we just gave them
money. They were nothing but clients, subjects. The people
who devised these programs were people of goodwill. But
they were basically saying, 'Here are a bunch of poor slobs
who are barely human; let's just give them a few bedrooms
and they'll be fine.'" Fuller's religiosity led him to believe, in
contrast, that "because it is the greater blessing to give than
to receive, recipients must also be allowed to give."

The Habitat ground rules are both traditional and revolutionary. In terms of housing policy, they represent a new
way to supply decent housing at the lower end of the economic spectrum. Rather than using public funds, Fuller relies on the combination of modest size, volunteer labor,
donated materials, and no-interest loans to lower costs to
the poor.

In terms of social policy, Fuller's ground rules are just as
significant. Habitat's screening of would-be homeowners
represents nothing less than a return to the nineteenth-
century concept of the deserving poor, though Fuller would
never use such language. His vision is truly that of a hand
up, not a handout—the phrase Lyndon Johnson used to announce his War on Poverty. Habitat's assistance is meant to
encourage and match the efforts of those being helped,
rather than to provide an entitlement based simply on

poverty. All this is in the great tradition of American charity—not just of the social gospel movement but also of the late nineteenth-century "scientific charity" movement, in which local private "charity organization societies" assessed the character of anyone who sought relief and required public service work in exchange, and of the settlement-house movement as well, with its emphasis on the middle-class values of thrift and cleanliness, and its hope of offering a venue in which rich and poor could meet.

For a family to become a Habitat homeowner, it must first agree to help build someone else's home, as well as to contribute labor to its own. The average requirement is 430 hours, or more than 10 full workweeks, per family. Willingness to match the labor of more affluent volunteers is by no means all that's asked of a partner family. It must be able to make a down payment of $100 as well as a monthly mortgage payment, often as low as $150 or $200, over a 20-year schedule. Most important, it must gain the approval of the local Habitat chapter's Family Selection Committee. The selection process is long and often difficult, say those who have served such committees. A family must establish need based on criteria ranging from lack of plumbing to overcrowding. (Habitat, setting its standards lower than HUD, does not consider two children sharing a bedroom to constitute overcrowding.) A family living in a shack, a broken-down mobile home, or a dangerous public housing project (notwithstanding the fact that its physical condition might be up to par) can qualify.

But need is not enough. A family must also pass what some local Habitat chapters explicitly label the criterion of "character." For example, West Virginia checks for the following traits:

"Steadiness: Family has not moved more than three times in the past ten years without good reason. Couple has been married at least one year.

"Care of Property: Living quarters were neat for interview. Family takes care of property and does not deface walls, break windows, etc.

"Interpersonal Relationships: Parents appear able to get along with others and would be an asset to a neighborhood. Children are well-behaved. Supervisor at work indicates family members get along with others."

In choosing its first twenty families, this chapter rejected sixty others. Habitat, moreover, continues to meet with partner families even after the house has been sold to them—both to help them deal with the responsibilities of home ownership and, if necessary, to remind them that if their payment does not arrive, they will lose their home. Cheryl Appline, the executive director of the Habitat chapter in poor, mostly black north central Philadelphia, makes no apologies about the strict enforcement of mortgage payments. "We must bring people into the world of real economic life. This is no giveaway." The group encourages upward mobility too. After only three years a Habitat family may sell its home, sharing whatever profit it realizes with the local chapter. (In contrast, federally subsidized single-family homes built through the federal Low Income Housing Tax Credit require fifteen years' residency before a renting family can even gain title to the home.)

Habitat's emphasis on values and character in selecting its families is in sharp contrast to what might be called the entitlement view of assistance expressed in such works as Francis Fox Piven and Richard Cloward's 1971 book *Regulating the Poor*—a view that had helped set the stage for the vast expansion of AFDC in the mid-sixties. In this view the poor are an undifferentiated victim group, surplus labor manipulated by the American economic system. They are no different from the middle class except for their lack of money. Millard Fuller, in contrast, is not shy about saying that "Habitat homes are not for everyone." And though staff members are skittish about drawing attention to the character issue—they emphasize that the organization is ecumenical and complies with all fair-housing laws (indeed, fully 56 percent of partner families are African American)—they acknowledge that they target the working poor. Household income ranges from $10,000 to $21,000, meaning that Habitat homeowners hold quite modest jobs. On a tour of Habitat houses in and around Charleston, West Virginia, I met owners who included a city garbage truck driver, a fast-food restaurant cook, a night-shift nursing home aide who also taught part time at a Christian school, and a clerk at a convenience store. A Habitat census of its partner families reflects its emphasis on character: only a third of Habitat households consist of single-parent families. By contrast, most of public housing families nationwide are female-headed.

Through its selectivity, Habitat has shown that it can be fiscally prudent to loan money to families of very modest means. Fully 89 percent of all Habitat families are completely current on their mortgage payments, a higher rate than for conventional mortgages. Even more impressive, since 1976 the organization's cumulative foreclosure rate has been less than 1 percent—a far better record than for federally subsidized programs for poor homeowners, which in the late sixties and early seventies had foreclosure rates as high as 35 percent. Habitat's low foreclosure rate surely has much to do with the emotional stake families have in homes they've physically helped to build. Even Jimmy Carter, whose administration emphasized rent subsidies for the poor, recognizes that Habitat families develop a "new sense of pride, dignity, and determination. They feel they've accomplished something on their own."

The Habitat approach contrasts with that of the federal Community Reinvestment Act, which requires banks to make capital available to "underserved" neighborhoods, based on the presumption that worthy applicants have been denied credit because of their race or zip code. The law provides an incentive for lenders to make loans easy to get: banks want to impress regulators with the sheer volume of capital being loaned. But lending money indiscriminately is a poor investment for banks and for neighborhoods alike. Habitat, by contrast, uses legitimate criteria to distinguish between good and bad credit risks at the very low end of the market—without discriminating on illegitimate bases such as race. Helping families who can make a solid commitment to their community, and who carry that commitment out by repaying their loans, is a far better way to rebuild poor neighborhoods than pouring in capital indiscriminately.

Habitat builds mostly in poor neighborhoods as a practical matter. Since it needs to keep its costs as low as possible, Habitat mostly buys or receives land in areas where it's cheapest. Moreover, the organization has encountered opposition in affluent neighborhoods, fueled by the assumption that Habitat housing would be similar to public housing. "They envision a housing project, a giveaway program, problems with drugs," says Susan Sewell, a Habitat officer. "When they learn it's ownership, the anxiety level may go down." But because American neighborhoods are organized on the basis of social class, such opposition is inevitable. And it is not Habitat's goal to force the rich to live with the poor. "We don't believe in trying to go where we're not wanted," says Fuller. This too is a significant departure from government social policy of the past quarter-century, including a recent HUD program that attempts to disperse subsidized renters in affluent and working-class suburbs and earlier, quixotic efforts to build "scattered-site" subsidized housing in places like Forest Hills, Queens, and middle-class parts of Yonkers. Such policies have consistently inspired middle-class resentment because they reward lack of income rather than work.

Habitat offers the hope of building self-sustaining poor neighborhoods with a strong core of homeowners. In Paterson, New Jersey, the local chapter has put up dozens of single-family houses on vacant land in that city's North Side ghetto, in what a *New York Times* account calls "an effort to create an entire neighborhood." This is the pattern among urban affiliates. In Sandtown, an impoverished black neighborhood in Baltimore, as well as in north central Philadelphia, local Habitat chapters have carved out specifically defined areas and begun the slow process of creating small outposts of owner-occupants within a desert of dilapidation. "Ownership is the only thing that stabilizes an area," observes Cheryl Appline, whose north central Philadelphia chapter plans to build or renovate fifty new houses a year within an eighteen-square-block area. "Owners sweep the pavement and shovel the snow and ice. They have a commitment to the area. Rental is a revolving door with no incentive to take care of the property."

Herein lies another revolutionary concept: a poor neighborhood can be a good neighborhood. Just as in middle-class communities, committed owner-occupants can maintain their homes well and keep their yards and sidewalks clean, help police keep the neighborhood safe, and even help teachers make the schools work. The ideas of ownership and community cohesion are missing in the much-discussed community development corporations, commonly supported by government and foundations in inner cities, which emphasize the physical renovation of existing structures, often as subsidized rental apartments, without attending to the reknitting of the social fabric that underlies any healthy neighborhood.

Despite its focus so far on rural towns and small cities, Habitat now aims to move in force into big cities—including New York, where its efforts to date have been pallid. In its recently announced "urban initiative," Habitat will have its national headquarters provide up to 70 percent of the funds for urban affiliates to build homes. (Ordinarily local chapters must raise construction funds on their own.) The urban initiative could direct millions of dollars to inner cities—and volunteer labor will stretch those funds further. Philadelphia's Appline boasts of more than five thousand volunteers ready to help; she estimates their labor will reduce Habitat construction costs by 25 percent, saving her chapter some $290,000 over two years and allowing her to sell new two-story, three-bedroom row houses for $60,000.

Habitat's fund-raising is, in the tradition of Fuller and Dees Enterprises, well organized and high-powered. Recognizing that its good name makes it an effective vehicle for corporate sponsorship, it works hard to attract such sponsors by promising, for instance, to direct their contributions into metropolitan areas where they are making a marketing push or opening new branches. And it deftly capitalizes on the self-sacrificing image of Jimmy Carter, volunteer, to raise funds; Carter himself sits on the Habitat board of directors and personally solicits major donors.

None of this would matter, of course, if Habitat did not manage to build decent houses that the working poor can afford to buy. As the Wal-Mart of social policy, Habitat provides a Wal-Mart-type product—the housing equivalent of good, cheap, unfancy clothing. Typical Habitat homes are strikingly modest by contemporary American standards: eleven hundred to twelve hundred square feet, two bedrooms, valued at $50,000. Contributed labor and materials bring the cost down to an average of $35,000.

But local governments multiply obstacles to Habitat's efforts to create low-cost, rather than merely low-income, housing. Housing construction in America is highly regulated by building and zoning codes, which can add significantly to the cost of construction. Habitat is pushing local authorities to question whether their regulations are necessary. It has locked horns with local authorities in south Florida over how thick the plywood it uses must be. Local officials are calling for five-ply thickness, in the name of hurricane safety; Habitat wants to save ten dollars a sheet by using three-ply wood, being willing to tolerate what it views as a minimal safety risk in order to keep the house within its target range. With some success, Habitat has urged local governments to reduce the fees paid for permits—a small matter for middle-class housing but far more important for a low-cost builder. It is currently embroiled in a dispute in Los Angeles as to whether it must build carports attached to its homes. Habitat wants to provide uncovered parking pads rather than adding 25 percent to its costs to build what its officials call a "house for a car."

Habitat's success suggests several questions. Why couldn't such housing construction simply be handled by private, for-profit firms, in the manner of most consumer goods? Or, conversely, if Habitat has been so successful through reliance on private donations, might it be able to accomplish even more with direct government support? And if Habitat helps the working poor, what does it do for the truly needy, those earning less than it takes even to own a Habitat home?

Doubtless private builders, freed from the kind of code, fee, and zoning requirements that Habitat opposes, could produce more housing for the working poor. But these onerous regulations arose because Americans have been uncomfortable with the idea of privately supplied, very modest housing for the poor. It seems exploitative for a de-veloper to profit by offering the poor cramped quarters without amenities, even if such housing is the first rung on the economic ladder. Habitat's emphasis on ownership makes the possibility of such upward mobility more real than does life in the rented shacks and tenements that give private low-income housing a bad name. Habitat's success in making the ownership of very modest housing the first step of upward mobility for many may spur localities across the country to revisit their zoning and building regu-lations, ultimately making it easier for responsible private-sector developers to build low-cost, low-income housing.

As for government funds, Habitat could not function as it does were it to take them. Building to federal standards for publicly supported housing would price its homes beyond the range of most partner families; subsidies would have to close the gap. Volunteers would not likely feel the same imperative if they believed that public funds could substitute for their labor. Still, government has helped Habitat indirectly, chiefly through the donation and preparation of land, and may be poised to do the same on a grander scale. A House subcommittee has approved $25 million in indirect federal aid to Habitat; Fuller is enthusiastic.

But such help would have its pitfalls. Although Habitat is scrupulous about conforming to fair-housing laws, an infusion of federal funds would inevitably place a spotlight on the subtle and subjective nature of its family selection process, laden with middle-class values, which, along with its zeal for low-cost construction, is the key to the Habitat formula. It may be that government can no longer distinguish appropriate from inappropriate discrimination. What's more, even though it may seem that only government can fund large-scale growth, Habitat has already grown phenomenally through corporate donations and direct-mail solicitation alone.

"The trick," says Fuller of government aid, "is to dance close to the snake but not to get bit." So far, so good: and perhaps Habitat can accept indirect HUD aid and maintain its independence. But, Fuller concedes, "all it takes is one lawsuit, no matter how little justification there is to it, to really tie us up in knots." A lawsuit directed at the organization's family selection process would be catastrophic. It may be that government could help Habitat most by figuring out how to get out of its way. Large-scale public support may be a temptation that this organization would do best to resist.

Habitat must resist, too, the notion that unless it houses even the poorest, most troubled welfare recipients, it is not really helping the poor. If the tragedy of American public housing—where the physical plant is often the least of the problems—has proved anything, it is that improved physical accommodations are not enough to uplift those at the bottom of society. To enter the mainstream economy, the very poor must move by small increments upward, with respect to both jobs and housing. Habitat, by providing a lower rung on the home ownership ladder to people of very modest means, also serves as a beacon of hope for those who cannot yet afford its homes. From the point of view of the projects, a nearby well-functioning neighborhood of poor but hardworking owners is something worth aspiring to.

Millard Fuller's books are filled with stories of the lives that Habitat has touched. True, they can be saccharine, but they're worth keeping in mind. One woman Fuller met in a public housing project told him that in public housing, "I feel all thronged away." A Chicago woman, in contrast, said that as a Habitat owner, "I now know how to put on a doorknob. I can fix a hole in the wall. I am getting ready to return to school, and I am looking forward to starting a new job. My children can now see life from a different view. Habitat has given me hope. I won't stop here; I will continue to move forward."

So, let's hope, will Habitat for Humanity.

[1995]

# Afterword

An organization like Habitat for Humanity points the way forward by showing how feasible it is to build housing for people at all income levels without government help. And even without the subsidy of private charity, the private market, especially if freed from needless regulation, is capable of turning out decent housing for all Americans. Thus the premise on which public housing rests—that in the all-important area of housing the private market necessarily fails—is simply false.

As for the promise of public housing—that better physical conditions would improve not only the material but also the moral lives of the poor—it hasn't come true. Like the open-ended welfare payments that welfare reform ended in 1996, subsidized housing, which still has no time limits attached to it, harms rather than helps those it sets out to assist by trapping them in dependency and enabling, even rewarding, dysfunctional behavior—especially having children out of wedlock.

Public housing hurts cities too, by reserving big tracts for modern-day poorhouses and preventing the creative recycling of land for new, vibrant uses. The housing projects that dominate many urban neighborhoods radiate blight, rather than vitality, outward into their surrounding neighborhoods.

Public housing also undermines the real achievements of those who, through hard work and perseverance, have risen out of the ranks of the poor, because it brings into their neighborhoods subsidized households lacking the incentive, and often the social skills, to keep the area well maintained and orderly. We must not fail to understand that the very characteristics that enable households to afford a better home in a better neighborhood—self-discipline, frugality, and marriage—are the same characteristics that undergird healthy communities.

Our task now is to dismantle public housing in a sensitive and humane way. Hundreds of thousands of Americans have made decisions based on the expectation that the present system will continue, so change must come gradually. The foundation of reform would be a limit on how long a household can stay in subsidized housing, and it is heartening to see that the Bush administration is taking the first steps in this direction. A time limit obligates households to take steps to prepare for life after public housing: which could mean finding a better job or getting married or even taking in a boarder to help pay the rent—the things Americans have always done to make ends meet and to get ahead.

At the same time, local policymakers need to remove every impediment—from unreasonable zoning restrictions to rent control—that prevents the market from building as much housing as is needed. The result of these changes will be vibrant neighborhoods, filled with good citizens, who care about and maintain both their property and the social order that makes a street of houses into a community of homes.

# Index

# A NOTE ON THE AUTHOR

Howard Husock is director of case studies at the John F. Kennedy School of Government at Harvard University, a position he has held since 1987. He is also a contributing editor to *City Journal* and director of the Manhattan Institute's project on social entrepreneurship. Before joining the Kennedy School, Mr. Husock was a public television journalist and Emmy award-winning documentary filmmaker. He lives in Brookline, Massachusetts.